Planning & Remodeling
Bathrooms

By the Editors of Sunset Books
and Sunset Magazine

Lane Publishing Co. • Menlo Park, California

Cover: *Vaulted ceiling—the axis connecting various areas in this remodeled bathroom—creates a centered space. Redwood and tile room began as side parlor, was next a closet. Large tub (see page 47) occupies one end of bathroom. Double basins and two shower heads save time; ample storage includes large cabinet with towel bar below (reflected in mirror). Architect: Robert Herman. Photographed by Edward Bigelow.*

Acknowledgments

The homeowners, architects, and designers who have improved that very personal part of the house, the bathroom, are the true authors of this book. We wish to thank them for their generous help both in sharing their experiences in bathroom design and construction and in "lending" us their bathrooms for photographs. Special appreciation goes to our consultant, architect Thomas A. Abels, and our resourceful photographer, Edward Bigelow.

Edited by Maureen Williams Zimmerman

Design: Roger Flanagan

Illustrations: Terrence Meagher

Title page: Shower heads fore and aft in quarry tile tub/ shower allow for thorough soaking. Steps lead into sunken tub; ledge at end holds plants. Architects: Clement Chen & Associates. Photographed by Darrow M. Watt.

Editor, Sunset Books: David E. Clark

Fourth Printing May 1977

Contents

Special Features

Revitalizing the bath

- **Decorate, remodel, or build?**
- **Getting help**
- **Money matters**
- **Plumbing**

Bathrooms are always with us, changing with the times and with our customs, fashions, and attitudes. History records that bathing was a religious ritual—a ceremonial purification—in ancient Egypt. Elaborate plumbing systems date from over 5,000 years ago in Crete. Homer's heroes are depicted as having bathed in tubs made from stone, marble, and wood.

Bathing as a matter of personal hygiene has had a checkered history—from the conviviality of public Roman baths, where more than a thousand citizens might bathe together, to the widespread abstinence from bathing in the Middle Ages. Even during the reign of Elizabeth I, few baths were found in houses, and the queen was reported to bathe only once a month. In fact, it wasn't until the Victorian era that bathrooms came to be separate rooms in the house. Even the White House didn't have a bathtub until after 1850.

Today, most of us feel that bathing and bathrooms are necessary and even enjoyable. But the particular type of bathroom that's right for you may be quite different from your neighbor's. Bath boutique shops and large sections of department stores devoted to bath accessories testify to the increased interest in improving and personalizing bathrooms. In many homes the master bath and master bedroom are integrated so that the bedroom, dressing room, and bath are combined to make a luxurious retreat. Gardening in the bathroom, and bathrooms with a view of a garden, are becoming more and more popular. Some bathrooms include a Finnish sauna or Japanese-style soaking tub.

Don't limit your thinking. Whether you are remodeling, redecorating, building, or buying, keep your mind open to new ideas—they may not be as expensive to actualize as you think, and the benefits may be great.

In this book we present many different styles and types of bathrooms. First, consider the ones that appeal to you most: what is it about them that you're responding to? Then pick out the aspects of these bathrooms that would be most useful and practical for you.

Ask yourself some general questions about the type of bathroom you would most enjoy. Do you visualize your bathroom as small and enclosed or as a large, open space? Will it be shared or private? Compartmentalized or a single room? Do you want to feel that you're indoors or out? Would you prefer a bright, sunny place or a cozy, dimly lighted place? Do you want a view or plain, close-up walls? Would you like lots of things to see and touch around you or a tidy, ascetic bathroom?

Other, more utilitarian needs should be met, too. The bathroom you're planning might be the only one in a house inhabited by several people. Or it might be one of several bathing and washing areas in a more lavish dwelling. The number of people who will be using a bathroom—their ages, individual habits, and needs—is information that's vital to your planning.

In your present bathroom, what are the features you don't like that should be changed? What do you plan to accomplish by redecorating, remodeling, or adding a new bathroom? If you're planning an entire new house, how will the bathroom relate to the rest of the house? What are your future needs?

After asking yourself these questions and as many similar ones as you can think of, you'll be ready to begin planning the bathroom that's right for you.

Will changes be extensive?

It's helpful to think of a bath redecoration or renovation or the construction of a new bath as an opportunity to achieve new comfort, beauty, and convenience. Simply adding new accessories or a fresh coat of paint can do much for the appearance of an old bathroom at a relatively small cost. New tiling or carpeting will rejuvenate an outdated bathroom; new shelves and cabinets can relieve irksome overcrowding.

For any type of change, begin by gathering as much information as you can on design ideas and the newest materials, fixtures, and accessories. Then work up a budget based on the parts of the job you think you can handle, the going local rate for skilled help, and the estimated cost of materials.

The answer may be decorating . . .

Though it's part of remodeling, decorating doesn't include structural changes. Its cost can range from modest to extravagant. Simple accessory changes can often revitalize a tired bathroom—a new color on the walls for an impression of spaciousness or brightness, or a new throw rug, shower curtain, and coordinated towels to add pattern. Certainly decorating is the quickest and most convenient way to visually change a bathroom.

Decorating is as individual as people. As in revamping any other part of the house, "rules" are made to be broken. However, some general guidelines that have proved successful for others may be helpful to you.

First, choose a background color for the walls, ceiling, and floor. Work around the existing fixture colors— match or complement them. The background color need not be the same tone on all surfaces. Changeable color accents in the room can be provided by matching or complementary towels, rugs, and other appointments. Consider color, pattern, and scale of all the bathroom components before making final decisions.

One aspect of bathroom decorating that's often overlooked is the relation of the bathroom colors to other rooms nearby. It's usually pleasing to decorate a small powder room in the same colors you're using in the adjacent foyer or entry hall or to coordinate a master bathroom color scheme with that of the master bedroom and possibly the dressing room.

. . . or is remodeling the approach to take?

Remodeling usually involves more than surface changes. Your goal might be a limited modernization or a dramatic rearrangement of space. The project could range from replacing tile and fixtures to enlarging an existing bathroom or converting a different type of room into a bathroom. Sometimes the addition (or subtraction) of a partition or wall will markedly transform a bathroom's overall appearance.

Homeowners may be surprised to find that remodeling can often cost more than adding on an entirely new bathroom. What contributes to the cost is the extra labor involved for demolition before beginning new building,

the restrictions of working within set measurements and structural elements, and—especially in older houses—the difficulty of knowing exactly what wires or other structural complications you're going to discover and then have to work around.

Many of the exciting features going into new bathrooms can be included in a remodeled one. But before you take a skylight idea from one source and a vanity design from another, make sure their designs work for the room as a whole—and that they work well with the design of the rest of the house.

In most cases the best way to begin remodeling is to draw a to-scale floor plan of your present bathroom, including the exact sizes and shapes of the fixtures. If the remodeled bathroom will include or affect other rooms, those rooms and their features should be on the floor plan, too. It's also helpful to make scale drawings of the walls. If you know the location of existing water supply and waste lines, you should include them, too.

Before you begin removing walls, plan the total project as completely as you can, down to details of locating ventilating ducts, heating ducts, light fixtures, storage cabinets, and mirrors. And calculate how much time it will take to complete your project, how to dispose of the materials and fixtures you tear out, and how to move such awkwardly shaped components as shower stalls and bathtubs in and out of your house.

To avoid the most common remodeling headaches, do these things: 1) Estimate time, money, and other factors as exactly as possible; 2) Know as much as you can about your community's plumbing and building codes, regulations, and guides (contact the city or county building department, mechanical and electrical inspectors); and 3) Have written agreements with whomever you employ to do work for you, including prices, general descriptions of fixtures and materials, and a statement that places on the installer the liability for an unsatisfactory installation or fixture damage.

Look for before-and-after examples of remodeled bathrooms on pages 8, 32-39, 61, 64.

If it's a new house

When you're planning a new house yourself or consulting an architect or designer, you have considerable choice in the location, type, and style of bathrooms. Of course, a bathroom's design shouldn't clash with the architectural style of the house.

Try to consider personal needs and desires you may have that might require more than the stereotyped, 5 by 8-foot, three-piece, standard bathroom package could provide. The standard package may be your ultimate choice, but don't settle for it without first looking into other possibilities.

Bathroom location theories vary. Where you locate your bathroom will be determined by available floor space, the needs of family members, and the number of bathrooms in the house. A common practice is to place fixtures back-to-back when two bathrooms are on the same floor, and above and below each other when they're on different floors. This way, plumbing can be shared by many fixtures. Doing this generally results in saving some money—but not always a large amount.

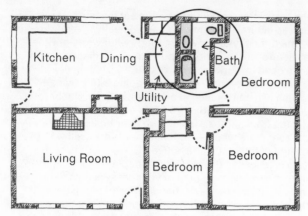

Typical placement *of single bathroom in one-story house.*

There are sound conceptual and economic reasons both for clustering sinks, baths, and toilets and for the alternative of separating them. Clustering is usually less expensive, but it might not be convenient or functional for you.

If the house will have only one bathroom, a logical choice is to position it between the public parts of the house (living room, entry) and the sleeping and dressing areas so that it is convenient to both sections. In a house that will have two or more bathrooms, placing one of them adjacent to a sleeping and dressing area is a popular choice.

In a 1½ or 2-story house, the bathroom is usually located on the second floor. For safety, avoid placing an upstairs bathroom next to or at the head of the stairs.

Building codes must be considered in planning bathroom location. For example, codes usually state that a bathroom can't open directly to a kitchen; the two rooms must be separated by a hallway or by two doors.

In a development house, your options on design, plumbing, fixtures, and other details depend upon the particular builder, his method of doing business, and, in some instances, how much you're paying for your house.

Some builders start with a basic plan and specifications and offer several options throughout the house, much as an automobile dealer will give you options of color, engine size, and so forth. Other builders—even those in the higher price categories—have developed standard plans for which they've organized purchasing and construction methods so they can build with maximum efficiency and economy. Because of the way they're organized, these builders can offer few, if any, options.

Getting the help you need

If you're redecorating you might consult an interior decorator; if you're remodeling you'll probably work with a carpenter and plumber; if you're building a new bathroom, you may employ a plumber, a contractor, and an architect.

Each of these specialists can help you by offering knowledge and skills that would take you years to acquire for yourself. Try to be aware of precisely what they can be expected to do for you, as well as what their limitations may be in relation to your specific project.

How much can you do yourself?

This is a question only you can answer. On the positive side, you can achieve great satisfaction by acquiring and using the skills you need, saving quite a bit of money, working at your own pace and at times that are convenient for you, and knowing the job was done with care and is up to your standards of excellence.

The negative aspects of doing the work yourself include the time you'd spend away from other activities that you enjoy more, the demands of having to solve vexing problems, the effort of learning the skills and estimating and buying the exact materials and tools you'll need, the possibly extensive physical labor of doing the work, and the potential need to hire someone to finish the job for you anyway.

Almost every remodeling project has a few easy, do-it-yourself opportunities. If you've done some projects before and enjoyed them, you can work on parts of the job yourself and leave other parts to specialists. But if your plans include plumbing, heating, air conditioning, or electrical work, be sure to check local ordinances before starting the work yourself. Permits will probably be required, and code compliance will be demanded. The regulations may require that certain portions of the job be done by licensed workmen.

For help in do-it-yourself projects, see manufacturers' instructions; these often are well illustrated and very complete. Many products on the home improvement market are specifically designed for installation by the homeowner. Since manufacturers and dealers want satisfied customers, they will probably be glad to answer specific questions. Your local government building department is another source of detailed and specific information. Articles and ads in home-oriented building and remodeling magazines can be helpful, and the *Sunset* books *Basic Carpentry Illustrated* and *Basic Plumbing Illustrated* are particularly good references.

Architects. . . and related professionals

An architect is a highly trained specialist in combining organization, esthetics, and practicality in construction. He designs and draws up plans for buildings and supervises construction.

If you're contemplating any kind of structural change, an architect can give you an individualized, custom design and save you time and money in the long run. He can help you with such things as how to get the most service out of the floor space, how to introduce natural light, how much storage to allot, and how to cope with bearing walls or other obstacles that might stand in the way of enlarging a bathroom.

You can employ an architect for all or part of a number of services. Here's what the architect will do: 1) Discuss and organize your basic needs and make rough sketches of practical solutions; 2) Draw up precisely detailed plans and specifications for bids, obtain the building permit for a new house (the contractor usually handles permits in remodeling), and ensure that nothing contradicts local codes and ordinances; 3) Supervise the contractor's work as it progresses, seeing that the requisite grades of materials and workmanship go into the job and that time schedules are met; and 4) Make a final inspection of the completed work and sign a certificate of approval when you and he are completely satisfied. Unless retained on a consultation basis specifying an hourly fee (the usual procedure in remodeling), architects generally work on a flat percentage basis tied in with the total cost of the job.

The best way to choose an architect is to inspect his work. Many licensed architects belong to a professional organization, the American Institute of Architects (AIA), which has a referral service. Look in the Yellow Pages under "Architects" for the address and telephone number of the nearest AIA chapter.

A building designer can be someone who has an architect's education and training but hasn't gone through the state's licensing procedure. Or he may be a member of a relatively new profession of building designers that has a separate educational program and a professional organization called the American Institute of Building Designers. The AIBD can refer you to a building designer on the basis of your location and the type of job you're contemplating. The national office is at 839 Mitten Road, Suite 206, Burlingame, CA 94010.

A building designer will provide you with preliminary drawings for a minor fee and a set of plans for a prearranged price. The designer will make constructive suggestions concerning your plan and help smooth out any rough edges.

A draftsman can be either an unlicensed, apprentice architect or a member of a skilled trade prepared to draw plans exactly according to your instructions. If you are experienced in building and know such things as which electrical conduits to specify, exact requirements for joists and studding, and the pros and cons of various fixtures, you could save money by hiring a competent draftsman at an hourly rate. To locate a draftsman, check the Yellow Pages under "Building Designers" or "Draftsmen."

A general or prime contractor

If your project will involve a number of subcontractors—such as plumbers, carpenters, electricians, tile setters—it might be to your advantage to use a reliable licensed general contractor. Contractors who do a large volume of work can buy materials for you at low wholesale prices. However, if the job is small, you may have difficulty finding a contractor willing to take it on because larger projects are more profitable for him.

In much of the bathroom remodeling being done, though, almost all of the work is handled by a single contractor/carpenter—a jack-of-all-trades who can carry out some plumbing tasks as well as carpentry.

Although doing your own contracting will certainly save you money, it will also eat up a lot of your time. You'll have to get in touch with, choose, and supervise the skilled workmen and cope with the fact that they often have strict union rules, such as a set working sequence.

To find a contractor or other skilled workers, talk with homeowners who have had work done. You can also check with subcontractors and material suppliers or a bank or local credit bureau.

When selecting a contractor, keep in mind that the one with the lowest bid is not necessarily the one who will do the job best. You should base your choice on his reputation in home building—he should be cooperative, competent, and financially solvent. He is the one who orders the materials and hires, supervises, and coordinates the work of the various subcontractors.

You should get in touch with at least two (and preferably three) contractors for a preliminary cost estimate on a major project. Though there is no fee or obligation of any kind on your part and no firm commitment on theirs, you'll have a basis for further planning.

After all major and minor decisions have been made, the contractor can give you a firm bid. Then a complete, legal, written contract should be prepared. The contract should include dimensions, specifications, and type and quality of all materials, as well as a time schedule, cleanup agreement, bankruptcy release, and payment agreement. Usually a contractor is paid either on the installment plan, voucher system, or in one lump sum upon completion. After you've made a thorough inspection, you acknowledge completion of the job in writing.

To build new tub, owner nailed exterior paneling to contoured extensions of wall studs, finished wood with fiberglass cloth and three sanded layers of resin.

Subcontractors: plumbers, tile setters, electricians

Whether or not to hire skilled workmen for all or part of the work is a decision that should be made early to avoid scheduling problems. If you plan to hire out most of the work, be sure you have the time and determination to act as your own general contractor; if not, hire a licensed one. The services of a plumbing contractor or other subcontractor include supplying current product information, selling fixtures and supplies, advising you, and doing work in accordance with technical drawings and specifications that comply with local codes.

At first glance the services of skilled workmen may seem expensive. Yet they have the specialized tools, training, and experience to finish the job much faster than you could, and you can expect a professionally finished job from them. Using skilled workmen can even save you money if you weigh it against the cost of your own time.

If you're acting as your own general contractor, you must know how to get the most from the people you hire. Often they're accustomed to the routine of doing a job in one particular way and do not welcome changes. For example, if you want the niche for the soap dish inset high in the shower wall to keep spray from the shower head from reaching it, you'll probably encounter resistance from the tile setter who wants to position the niche where he's used to putting it.

Trade associations can recommend licensed subcontractors on the basis of your location and the type and extent of work involved. Check the Yellow Pages under "Plumbing Contractors," "Electric Contractors," and "Tile-Ceramic, Contractors" for the address and telephone number of the local branch of the trade association. Recommendations from other homeowners will also help you to locate subcontractors.

When dealing with subcontractors, make sure you supply clear instructions, have all firm agreements in writing, know what's realistic to expect, and provide as much direct supervision as you can.

An interior decorator or designer

These specialists in the decorating and furnishing of interiors offer professional skill in making the most of what you have. Beyond that, they supply fresh, innovative ideas and interpretations and provide access to unique materials and products.

Usually, homeowners contact a particular interior designer on the basis of personal recommendations or because they've seen and liked work by the designer in magazines, books, or at a show house. Membership in a professional organization called the American Society of Interior Designers (ASID) is one assurance that a designer is well qualifed. Check the Yellow Pages under "Interior Decorators & Designers" for the telephone number and address of the ASID chapter in your area.

Interior designers work on a very individual basis; their approaches often differ, too, according to the type and size of a specific job. A preliminary interview is customary to see whether the homeowner and the designer can work together effectively, communicating about each other's taste and ideas. Interior designers usually either charge a professional fee (hourly rate) or take a percentage of the cost of the merchandise used.

Before (below): Shower stall on left was removed, as was built-in chest on outside wall. **After** (right): Space under the house and low drainage lines allowed the tub to be recessed and placed against new window wall.

8

How much bathroom can your money buy?

The amount of money you spend determines, to a certain extent, the bathroom you'll end up with. The most obvious effect of economics on the bathroom is its standard 5 by 8-foot size. Then, too, a certain amount of standardization has been necessary in the bathroom fixture industry to keep costs down. But creating an outstanding, out-of-the-ordinary bathroom doesn't have to be a severe strain on your budget.

How to calculate expenses

Early in your planning, you should determine the amount of money you can reasonably afford to spend in building a new bathroom or redesigning an existing one, based on discussions with a building designer, architect, or contractor. Keep in mind your plans for the future. Along with present expense, consider future mortgage and later remodeling possibilities. With a new bathroom, your house will be more valuable. A new bathroom may be the first stage of a long-term remodeling project.

It's wise to prepare a complete budget and list of materials before you buy anything. The time you spend researching costs and calculating specific prices will save you time and money later.

On the list of materials, include an implementation schedule and the exact cost of the materials you need. Select alternatives to your first choices—you may find a particular item has been discontinued or is available only after a months-long wait. Time is perhaps the most difficult cost factor to estimate for each phase of work and for the whole project; this is particularly true if you're planning to do part of the work yourself.

To determine costs accurately, refer to a scaled floor plan and wall elevations to calculate the exact quantities of materials you'll need. A mail order catalogue and a few telephone calls can give you quick price estimates. Describe your entire project; if the total cost of materials is substantial, the supplier will probably offer a discount. In most instances the cost of labor will be from 60 to 75 percent of the total cost of materials, but a reputable local contractor can give you a more precise estimate based on your materials list.

The sales tax on building materials shouldn't be overlooked in planning costs—it may be substantial. It's deductible from your income tax when you're acting as your own contractor.

Financing your new bathroom

An important consideration in most extensive bathroom remodeling and building projects is how to finance the work. The ideal way is to anticipate the project a few years in advance, open a special savings account, and deposit a given amount monthly. This allows you to begin your project when your target date arrives, saving you a substantial amount of interest.

Loans of various types for home improvements are available from several sources. Because terms and interest rates vary from one locality to another and sometimes from bank to bank in the same community, it's worthwhile to shop around.

Commercial banks, savings banks, and savings and loan companies are usually the best places to consult. Consider especially FHA home improvement loans available through these sources and other special loan programs sponsored by local or federal government agencies. A loan arranged through a contractor is usually more costly than a loan taken out directly by the property owner.

Other possibilities include borrowing against a life insurance policy or from a company credit union and mortgaging or remortgaging a house.

Once you have a rough idea of how complicated the construction job will be, you can confer with a loan officer. Although at this stage the lending institution won't be able to commit itself on exact amount, terms, or interest, the loan officer can give you the bank's "rule of thumb" regulations governing modernization loans. Since each institution has its own rules governing the amount and length of loan and rate of interest, investigate thoroughly before making your final decision. When you have a completed set of plans and a specific bid on the work, you can settle exact arrangements.

Plumbing—underneath it all

Behind (and underneath) every successful bathroom is some plumbing. An understanding of the mechanics of a plumbing system will help you better plan a new bathroom or a remodeling project. (For more detailed answers to plumbing questions and for information on do-it-yourself plumbing, consult the *Sunset* book *Basic Plumbing Illustrated*.)

Know your plumbing system

"Plumbing" includes all the piping and piping accessories needed to bring water into and through the house and then take water out of the house. Each plumbing fixture is connected to a supply of water. Each of these fixtures is also connected to a drain system that carries the used water away.

The basic in-out circuit becomes more complex when a fixture requires both hot and cold water and when several fixtures are connected to the same supply and drain pipes. In addition, if the drainage system is to function correctly, it must be vented to the atmosphere through special vent pipes. These vent lines increase the apparent complexity of the overall system.

Supply. A house's water supply system consists of pipes and fittings in carefully planned sizes, assembled on the job site or prefabricated in a shop.

A supply main carries water under pressure into the house from the public water main outside. Then the supply main delivers the water to one or more supply branches or risers, which in turn divide at the water heater into hot and cold-water subsystems. Pipes for the two usually run parallel throughout the house. The supply main contains a house shutoff valve and a water

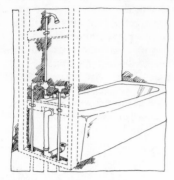

Money-saving plumbing hints

As you plan, be aware of plumbing economies. In the total budget of a house—and to an even greater extent in a remodeling project—plumbing is an expensive item. Generally, fixtures, fittings, and labor will cost more than lines of pipe.

Here are some ways to economize as you're planning the plumbing:

• Place new fixtures close to existing pipes to minimize extra carpentry and plumbing.

• Locate kitchen plumbing on one side of a common wall and bathroom plumbing on the other.

• Do as much work as possible at one time, while the pipes in the walls are exposed.

• Have existing plumbing checked for weakness, catching trouble before it starts.

• If you anticipate future changes, rough in the pipes to avoid opening walls a second time.

• If possible, plan upstairs and downstairs plumbing on the same wall, again to save extra pipes and carpentry.

• Use qualified plumbers who guarantee the results. If you're doing the job yourself, remember that plumbing must pass the local building department's inspection. Otherwise, you may have to rip it out and do it over again.

See an architect, designer, builder, or plumbing contractor for additional money-saving possibilities. If you want to save by doing your own plumbing, see the *Sunset* book *Basic Plumbing Illustrated* for detailed directions.

meter. The branches and risers have individual room shutoff valves marked "hot" or "cold."

• *Hot-water systems.* These are of two basic types. In one, the water is heated instantaneously in a boiler and continuously circulated in a loop pipe system by a pump to give immediate hot water at the outlet. In the other type, water is heated and then stored in a tank for future use. The need for hot water is usually estimated to be one-third of the need for cold water.

• *Pipe materials.* Galvanized steel is the traditional material for water pipes. Copper tubing, though usually more expensive per foot, is also widely used since it is normally easier to install. Plastic pipe is easiest for a do-it-yourselfer to work with. In addition, it doesn't corrode, it insulates well, and it may be less expensive than other kinds of pipe. The disadvantages of plastic pipe are its noisiness and a tendency to sag. Then, too, some local building codes don't allow plastic pipe, or they allow it only for drain-waste-vent lines.

• *Exposed pipes.* Although plumbing is usually concealed, it doesn't have to be. Left exposed, it can suggest the kinetic processes that make the house work; it can also be the basis for decorative experiment. In Europe, exposed hot-water pipes are often used as towel racks/warmers. The main drawback to exposed

plumbing is added expense—it must have a more finished appearance than concealed plumbing.

Drain-waste-vent. Used water leaves each fixture through a drainpipe, which is part of the system that handles water drainage, waste removal, and venting.

At each fixture the drain passage contains a U or S-shaped bend called a "trap." This trap retains water that acts as a seal to prevent gases and bacteria from entering the house.

Each fixture is also vented—connected to vertical pipes (stacks) that carry off sewer gases, bring in fresh air, reduce corrosion, and keep the whole drain-waste-vent system at the atmospheric pressure necessary to maintain the water seal in each trap. Vent stacks extend through the roof, where they open to the air.

The toilet vent pipe, called the "soil stack," often serves also as the main vertical waste line. The term "wet venting" is applied to this system for venting and draining waste water through the same vertical pipe. Revents or back vents connect secondary vents from other fixtures to the soil stack above the level of the highest fixture in the house. The soil stack connects with the main house drain in the basement or crawl space.

The main house drain is a large horizontal pipe that transports used water and wastes from the soil stack and other drainpipes to the house sewer outside. Since the waste and drainpipes work by gravity, they must be planned and fitted with special care. Strict code requirements govern pipe size, vent/fixture offset, and other factors.

When you're replacing fixtures

As a preliminary step, it's a good idea to consult a plumbing contractor to determine whether or not the existing piping will work satisfactorily with the new fixtures you're considering. Sometimes the age and condition of existing piping require that it, too, be replaced along with the bathroom fixtures.

Even if the pipes are in good shape, you're likely to run into some snags if you live in a house that's more than 15 or 20 years old. If new fixtures have slightly different dimensions, you'll have to make some changes in the house's internal plumbing as well as at the outlet.

See the information about each specific type of fixture (pages 24-28) for additional hints.

Installing and extending plumbing

Installing plumbing for a house addition or converting a room to an extra bathroom involves installation of water-supply and drain-waste-vent piping in walls, floors, and ceilings. This preliminary work is called "roughing in."

If you're going to extend existing plumbing, try to work around the existing waste lines and soil stacks. Relocating them can be very costly and, in some instances, virtually impossible. In a home built on a concrete slab, for example, the waste lines and base of the soil stacks are embedded in the concrete and would have to be cut out to relocate the fixtures. In homes with crawl space or sufficient area under the bathroom floor, these lines can be relocated, but it's an expensive process.

The maximum wet-vented distance between the fixture trap outlet and the soil stack is specified by the National Plumbing Code according to pipe diameter; however, each community has its own rules and regulations. Always plan piping layouts to take the most direct route, avoiding obstacles wherever possible.

Factory-made plumbing core. In some areas you may be able to purchase a factory-made plumbing core that will provide ready hookups for bathroom, kitchen, and laundry fixtures. These prefabricated sections are sometimes open-stud walls that are quickly nailed in place as a plumbing wall of a house. In other instances these cores are complete rooms that are lowered onto subflooring to provide both a finished bathroom and plumbing hookups for kitchen fixtures. Local builders and building supply firms can tell you whether these units are available in your area and whether they conform to the local building code.

Water pressure. It's advisable to check available water pressure when planning an additional bathroom. One way to do this is to turn on several faucets in the house for a few minutes. If the pressure drops noticeably, the outside water supply may be inadequate and larger pipes may be needed. Or deposits in the old supply pipes may reduce available pressure, necessitating replumbing the house supply system.

Hot-water supply. Another factor to consider in remodeling a bathroom or adding another is the size of your water heater and its recovery rate. An average 2½-bathroom house with an automatic washer and dishwasher requires at least a 50-gallon hot-water tank. Each manufacturer of hot-water supply tanks has his own method of calculating the storage capacity of tanks for families of different sizes and different hot-water demands. They all publish tables that can be used to judge the size of the tank required.

Future needs. Anticipating future remodeling when you're building a new house can save you money later. For example, if you intend to eventually finish a basement as a family room with half-bath or to add an attic bedroom and bathroom sometime in the future, you can run plumbing to the area, cap it, and wait to install fixtures later. Roughing in plumbing during initial construction is cheaper than adding supply and drain-waste-vent installations in a finished house.

Plumbing codes differ

Every community's building codes are different. A book of suggested guidelines—the *Uniform Plumbing Code*—might help answer some of your plumbing questions. *The Uniform Building Code* is another good reference; your local laws may be stricter, though.

Most areas require ventilation for an interior bath and, in some areas, a marble slab as the toilet base, marble baseboard trim, and ceramic floor tile laid over metal lath and mortar. In some cases the latter requirements are waived on the basis of an "existing condition." But you may find yourself having to put down a ceramic tile floor first before you can lay carpeting.

It's wise to have your own copy of the local written regulations and to ask the building inspector specific questions before beginning your project.

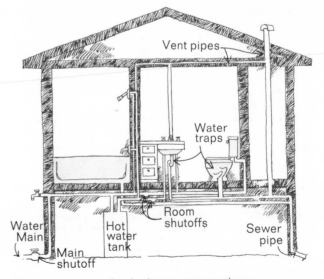

Basic components of a plumbing system are shown.

The comfort factors

- **Natural lighting**
- **Electric lighting, wiring, outlets**
- **Heating**
- **Ventilation**
- **Soundproofing**

A comfortable, functional bathroom depends on good lighting, ventilation, heating, and sound control. Maintaining a desirable physical atmosphere in a bathroom calls for certain special approaches.

Windows and skylights

These panels of glass or plastic connect a walled-in bathroom with what's outside, and this connection—which functions in both directions—affects the bathroom's light level, movement of air, temperature, visual effect, and auditory effect. Without windows, mechanical bathroom ventilation is a necessity.

Opening windows can cool off a hot, steamy bathroom. Windows can bring in a garden view and garden sounds. In addition, the natural light from windows and skylights, coupled with bathroom humidity, will encourage plants to thrive in your bathroom, adding to its attractiveness. Reflections and views from windows and strategically placed skylights can make a bathroom seem much larger than its actual size.

About glass and plastic

You'll find many kinds of glass and plastic to choose from for bathroom windows and skylights. Each type has its special purposes, its own advantages and disadvantages. If you use tinted, patterned or stained glass, pay particular attention to its effect on your total decorating and color scheme. Degree of light transmission and heat gain and loss are the most important features to consider. In specific locations where safety is a factor, local building codes will probably define the kind of glass to be used.

Clear glass. Standard clear and transparent window glass brings the maximum amount of daylight—as much as 88 to 90 percent of what's outside—into the bathroom. It's the most common and least expensive type of glass.

Insulating glass. Insulating glass consists of two sheets of glass with a dry gas or dry air space sealed between them. The outer sheet of glass may be tinted.

Usually, an insulating glass unit with 1/2-inch air space will reduce heat loss through the glass area by about one-half. Just as insulating glass will block some heat loss from the bathroom on cold days, so will it also reduce heat input on hot days. To further reduce heat transmission, order the glass with a reflective surface.

Insulating glass will reduce condensation, also. By keeping indoor glass surfaces warmer on cold days, it permits indoor humidity levels to go quite high without causing condensation. New types of insulating glass with a special reflective coating insulate like three sheets of glass, permitting still higher indoor humidity before condensation occurs.

Reflective glass. From the outside, reflective glass has a mirrorlike appearance. But from the inside you can see through it. Such glass cuts down the amount of heat transmission by as much as 70 percent while reducing light transmission by 50 to 70 percent. It also reduces glare and ultraviolet transmission.

You can have an aluminum-coated polyester film applied over the inside of already-installed clear glass areas to increase reflection and thus reduce solar transmission. The manufacturers claim it rejects 75 percent of the sun's heat and about 80 percent of the glare.

Tinted glass. This type of glass blocks much solar radiation—though part of it is soon reradiated to the inside as heat. Tinted glass also provides more privacy than clear glass, with little impairment of the view to the outside.

How much does tinted glass alter colors? When you're looking outdoors from within, gray-tinted glass provides very natural color retention. Bronze may make the outdoors appear slightly brighter while actually reducing light intensity, but most people observing the outdoors through it will be unaware of any change in color. Green-tinted glass slightly intensifies green colors and tends to make the outdoors look cooler.

It's possible to apply a tinted coating to glass in existing windows. Several companies manufacture spray-on or flow-on tinting products that reduce both glare and solar heat and repel fabric-fading ultraviolet rays.

Patterned glass. You can use this type of glass in a bathroom where good light is required yet privacy is important. The degree of privacy is determined by the pattern you choose; many patterns and textures are available. Patterned glass is also desirable because of its light-diffusing properties. If safety is a factor, use tempered or wired patterned glass. Patterned glass is also available in colors and with a glare-reducing finish. Plastic panels come in patterns, too.

Stained glass. This glass is used primarily for its interplay of color and light; stained glass also ensures privacy. Color, style, and subject matter of stained glass panels vary widely. Blown glass is more expensive and has richer color with more variations of shade and thickness than machine-pressed glass.

Sound control glass. Made with thick plastic layers laminated between two sheets of glass, sound control glass reduces sound transmission.

Safety glass and plastic. Most communities require that safety glass or plastic be used in all areas that could be hazardous, such as framed and unframed sliding glass doors, fixed glass panels less than 18 inches above the adjacent floor (they could be mistaken for doors), and shower doors and tub enclosures. Materials specified include fully tempered glass, wired glass, laminated glass, and rigid plastic. These won't break readily—and if they do, the chances of bad cuts are minimal.

• *Tempered glass.* This glass is three to five times stronger than untempered glass of the same kind and thickness, and not much more expensive. You can get tempered glass in sheet or plate, clear or patterned, plain or tinted types. Measurements for custom tempered glass must be exact; the material can't be recut once it goes through the tempering process.

• *Wired glass.* Wire mesh incorporated in the glass holds it together if broken. It's widely used (and widely required) in skylights. There are several different wire patterns.

At night, *glass panes coated with reflective, metalized polyester film become usable overhead mirrors.*

During daylight hours *you can see out through a comfortably "tinted" window (below), but people outside can't see in (right). The metallic film reduces heat, glare, and fading caused by the sun's ultraviolet rays. Architect: Pat Coplans.*

Generous fixed panes of glass, plants create feeling of showering outdoors. Architect: Carl Day.

Corner window of mitered glass overlooks private yard. Architect: Raymond L. Lloyd.

Shoji screen made from plastic panels hinged to old window frame allows light and privacy.

• *Laminated glass.* Clear or tinted vinyl is sealed between two pieces of clear or patterned glass. If the glass is broken, the plastic inner layer holds the glass together. Cost is high and not competitive with that of tempered sheet glass for residential installations.

• *Plastic.* Rigid clear, patterned, or tinted panels with a high shatter resistance are often used in windows, room dividers, doors, and skylights. Sizes and thicknesses vary. Plastic panels aren't as cleanable or abrasion resistant as glass, but they're less likely to shatter and easier to work with and install.

How to use windows

To give maximum benefit, windows should be thoughtfully placed, and they should be the right size and style for the particular bathroom. For example, it often isn't practical to put a large window over a bathtub, for the window will be difficult to reach to open and close and can cause drafts. If windows are used over a tub, they should be installed high enough to allow privacy and also be above the shower spray level.

A bathroom window should be easy to open and close for ventilation and temperature control, and it should be screened to keep out insects.

Windows on southern and eastern sides of a house bring in more light and solar heat; the north and west sides will receive less intense sunlight. West sun can be the most difficult to handle; east sun is the most desirable because it warms the bathroom in the morning.

You could try windows on two bathroom walls for cross ventilation. But try to avoid having bright light streaming through a window directly onto a mirror.

Window styles. Windows for a bathroom can slide horizontally (generally the most economical), slide vertically (double-hung), swing from the side (casement), swing from the top (awning), or pivot vertically (projected).

Some architects have made a point of separating fixed glass—for seeing through—from the opening for air, which then comes through separate louvers. If you plan a garden next to the bathroom, you could open an entire wall to the view with a combination of fixed glass and a sliding glass door and screen.

Generally, maintenance of bathroom windows is easier if they have aluminum rather than wood frames, particularly in climates where sticking and swelling can be a problem.

Window decoration. Window treatments of many sorts can be used in the bathroom. Among the possibilities are shutters or louvers, Roman shades, woven blinds, or curtains. The only real limitation is that ruffly, delicate materials tend to suffer from humidity. Tightly woven fabrics like duck, sailcloth, and denim are sturdier.

Various devices can be used to call attention to a glass area that might be a safety hazard. Decals come in many designs; paste-on muntin strips running horizontally across a door or window, two to four feet above the floor, are easy to see, especially if they are 2 or more inches wide and metallic or brightly colored.

Plants, chairs, or open storage units are effective in front of glass walls and windows. Mobiles, hanging panels of stained or colored glass, or wire sculptures are decorative in front of glass panels and call attention to them as well.

Should you add a skylight?

Skylights are an exciting way to bring in natural light and open up the bathroom visually, especially if you have a windowless interior bathroom or privacy problems. Skylights combined with windows can create exciting effects.

You can avoid the three possible problems with skylights—leaks, heat loss, and difficult maintenance—if you choose the skylight carefully.

Types. Check your local building codes regarding approved kinds of glass and plastic, how much area the skylight can cover, and other possible restrictions. Skylights are available in clear and colored plastic and in glass domes as well as in glass block units set in frames. Most residential skylights are manufactured in units complete with frames. Commercial greenhouse sections make great skylights, offering variety of design and the option of opening and closing. Successful installation, though, may be more difficult.

Translucent plastic domes are the most common form of factory-made residential skylights. They cut down the strong light that a clear skylight would admit to a room, and the domed shape tends to be cleaned by rainfall. On the other hand, clear skylights are effective if you want to look up at the clouds or at tall trees, and they admit about 85 to 92 percent of available light.

Flat glass or plastic skylights are sometimes used on sloping roofs, but they increase the amount of glare and heat in the bathroom unless they admit only north light. A flat skylight requires more cleaning than a domed one.

Condensation on the inside of a skylight can be a problem in winter or in cold climates; double-glazed dome skylights prevent condensation and also reduce heat loss. Most skylights have gutters to drain off condensation. In a windowless bathroom, use of a ventilating fan will lessen the skylight condensation problem.

Installation. Proper installation of a skylight is essential—otherwise it's almost sure to leak. Some units can be purchased ready for installation, requiring only that you cut a hole in the roof, set the skylight in place and anchor it, and then install the roofing material over the skylight roof flange.

If a skylight is oriented east or north on a sloping roof, it won't let in much hot afternoon sun. In cases where a skylight must face south or west, a shade or blind can be used to reduce heat and light intensity.

Electric lighting, wiring, outlets

Bathroom lighting should be both practical and decorative. Good lighting can create a feeling of spaciousness; an otherwise cramped, drab bathroom can be made to seem larger and more inviting through a change in the lighting arrangement.

Plans for lighting the bathroom should begin in the blueprint stage of a remodeling project because lighting is difficult and expensive to add later. To keep costs

Sunshine *from small skylight floods through warm golds and ambers of stained-glass panel. Designer: Robert Wendt.*

down, don't change light fixture locations—behind-the-walls rewiring is costly. When new light fixtures are added, it's advisable to have an electrician verify that the new unit won't overload the existing circuit.

Bathroom lighting falls into two basic categories: general illumination of the room as a whole and lighting for specfic areas. The two should be balanced to avoid glare. A light level of 30 footcandles is recommended by engineers for bathroom lighting. In nontechnical terms, this is the equivalent of 3.5 to 4 watts of incandescent lighting per square foot of floor area or 1.5 to 2 watts of fluorescent lighting.

Overall illumination

Diffused, ambient, overall lighting helps prevent glare. The source of general lighting can be a complete luminous ceiling, a luminous panel, track lighting, or a single, effective ceiling fixture. Ceiling fixtures are often quite decorative and can be combined with a vent fan or with an infrared heat lamp.

The safest way to handle overhead lighting is to wire it to a switch just outside the bathroom door.

Relation to room decor. The colors and textures used within the bathroom have an important effect on the lighting. Dark colors absorb light; white fixtures and light walls reflect and diffuse light, reducing shadows.

If there's a lot of contrast between light and dark in your bathroom, you should try to compensate by raising the amount of general light. Do this with additional fixtures rather than with brighter bulbs. Be especially careful that wattage isn't too strong if you're using shiny, glossy, and metallic-look wallpapers.

Use wall, ceiling, and floor surfaces in your lighting plan—they reflect and diffuse light, helping to control the actual amount of light. Matte surfaces reflect a pleasing, diffused light that is generally glareless. Some wood interiors, such as paneling and cabinets, can be bleached or given a light wash of paint to improve their reflective qualities without hiding the grain. If you have a lot of light-swallowing dark surfaces, you'll have to add enough light to overcome the lack of reflection.

Luminous ceiling. When the entire ceiling is the light source, there are few if any shadows and the bathroom seems more spacious. The luminous panels and grid supports are ideal for lowering a too-high ceiling or hiding ceiling imperfections.

A luminous ceiling usually consists of fluorescent tubes or incandescent bulbs attached to the ceiling, a grid of aluminum or wood strips 6 to 12 inches below the tubes or bulbs, and plastic or glass panels set into the grid. Luminous ceilings can usually be hung with nothing more sophisticated than hand tools. This type of lighting can be purchased as a packaged unit or it may be custom designed. Some packages come complete with heaters and ventilating fans for installation as one unit.

Single luminous panel. A circular or rectangular luminous panel can be attached to a regular electrical outlet in a ceiling for streamlined wide-source lighting.

Track lighting. Versatile track lights can be adjusted to reflect off walls for diffused illumination or to spotlight a particular area where you need more light.

Single ceiling fixture. Single-source lighting arrangements can work well in a small bathroom. A chandelier or other distinctive fixture can be used decoratively.

Localized lighting

Different fixtures have been developed for the different areas in the bathroom that have special lighting requirements. Mirrors—which are usually located over the sink—have the most specific requirements. Tub and shower enclosures also require special lighting.

If the bathroom is compartmentalized, each compartment should be well lighted, which means an additional light over the toilet. Special bath adjuncts—such as gym equipment, saunas, and steam rooms—may require special illumination.

Don't make localized lighting too bright. If you can't look directly at the fixture, or if you see an afterimage when you look away, the lights are too bright. Use diffusing methods such as frosted bulbs or frosted glass or plastic panels, or bounce the light off a wall. Better yet, install additional sources of lesser-intensity light.

At the mirror. Light for grooming should be soft and diffuse, without glare or shadows. Mirror lighting should be directed toward the person in front of the mirror rather than toward the mirror itself. Lights that shine directly on the mirror tend to blur the image and give dazzling reflections. Lights along both sides of the mirror, in addition to a ceiling downlight, will usually give an accurate mirror image. The lighting from the sides is important—overhead lighting alone can cause deceptive shadows.

Lighting above the mirror might be a row of bulbs (theatrical lighting), a long fluorescent tube or incandescent bulbs behind a diffusing panel or on a soffit, or a single decorative fixture. Extra lighting above the mirror is really necessary only if the general overhead light is less than adequate or if the side lights are far apart.

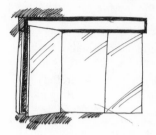

Diffusing panel *softens light from fluorescent tubes or incandescent bulbs, can be used for side-lighting, too.*

When one or two basins are installed in a vanity counter more than four feet wide, try several 75-watt incandescent bulbs or two rows of fluorescent tubes running the length of the mirror and counter, installed on a soffit that's at least 15 inches from front to back.

The lights on the sides of the mirror can be vertically mounted tubes behind diffusing plastic or glass, a row of bulbs, or other fixture style that suits the bathroom's decor. In most cases, side lights can be added without changing the wiring. Widely available surface-mounted fixtures can be wired into the existing fixture. Swag lights use a decorative chain to disguise obvious cords.

Theatrical lighting—*rows of bulbs first used in actors' dressing rooms—supplies an accurate, shadowless reflection.*

The decorative effect you want and the degree of efficiency you need will influence your choice of light fixtures. Ordinarily, all three light fixtures—the one above and the two beside the mirror—are controlled from one wall switch.

Tub and shower lighting. An auxiliary light is a good idea for most tubs and showers, especially if you have opaque doors or a heavy shower curtain. Special moisture and steam-resistant light fixtures, circular or rectangular, can be recessed into the ceiling over the shower or tub. These lights must be UL approved for use in tub and shower areas. Be sure to place the light switch so it's out of reach of someone using the tub or shower.

Toilet light. If your bathroom is compartmentalized, you'll need an additional light for the toilet enclosure. In either an open or a compartmentalized bathroom, a reading light is also convenient. A wall source or ceiling down-light with a 50-watt incandescent bulb usually works well. Rewiring might be necessary if you add a toilet light.

Incandescent or fluorescent lighting?

This choice depends on the general effect you want to create in your bathroom, the need for bright light in certain parts of the room, and your personal preferences. Incandescent bulbs provide the most flattering light; fluorescent tubes produce more light at less wattage, conserving energy.

Incandescent bulbs are more like sunlight in effect. White bulbs are usually best for bathrooms because tinted bulbs or shades can distort colors.

Fluorescent tubes extend light in a line. Check with a dealer to find out which kinds are best for use in a bathroom. Fluorescent bulbs come in different shades, some more flattering to skin tones than others.

As a pleasant compromise, a combination of incandescents and fluorescents can create a soft but adequate glow throughout the room.

Special types of lights and lamps

Some lights are combined with a fan, heating element, or both; others can be connected with a sun lamp. Check for special wiring codes that must be followed for heat lamps or sun lamps.

Heat lamps are ideal for instant warmth when you step out of a shower or tub. They'll heat a bathroom during the cooler portions of seasons when the regular house heating is turned off. Follow the manufacturer's recommendations when installing and operating heat lamps.

Ozone lamps aid in freshening the air. These lamps should be mounted above eye level, as they should not be viewed directly.

Sun lamps can help you keep a year-round tan. Follow the manufacturer's recommendations for installation and use of the lamps. You might investigate ceiling fixtures that include fans, ultraviolet heat, and sun lamps. Several manufacturers make combination fixtures that permit sunbathing while one shaves or dresses, with timers as auxiliary devices to guard against overexposure. These fixtures can be recessed into the ceiling.

Night lights are helpful in any bathroom to prevent stumbling in the dark, and are especially practical in children's bathrooms. Dimmers are available to provide varying levels of light. With fluorescent lighting, special dimming ballasts are required.

Electric outlets

While you're planning your wiring, be sure to consider outlets for all the electric appliances you might want to

*Platform behind bathtub folds down (above) to allow sunbathing under ultraviolet and heat lamps. Large acrylic skylight provides a view. **Unobtrusive** platform (right) folds up, disappears in wall. Architect: Brett Hanville.*

Small fireplace *warms bathroom for bathers, removes steam condensation from mirrors. Architect: Fred Hummel.*

use in your bathroom. These may include electric shavers, electric toothbrushes, hair dryers, curlers, and facial saunas. Think about storage for these appliances at the same time you're planning the electric outlets. Will they be out on the counter or in a vanity or medicine cabinet near the outlet?

Heavy-duty outlets for heaters and other equipment that draw considerable current should also be planned in advance.

All electric installations must be in accordance with local electric codes, and electric appliances should be used with caution. Codes usually require a minimum of one grounded electric outlet (near the basin) per bathroom.

Safety considerations

Switches for lights should be located so that they can't be operated by anyone using the tub, shower, or lavatory. Placing a switch for an overhead light just outside the entrance to the bathroom is a good idea. The electrical cords for any appliances used in the bathroom should be in top condition, and a grounded connection should be provided for use with electric appliances.

Any changes made to the lighting system must conform to the local electric code requirements. Every

bathroom has the potentially dangerous combination of water and electricity, so follow every precaution.

Heating your bathroom

What could be worse for early risers than a cold and drafty bathroom? Be sure the heating arrangements will be adequate. Pay special attention to the areas where heat loss will be greatest: along exterior walls and in front of exterior doors and windows.

For extra luxury, some people like to step out of a tub or shower into the warmth provided by a nearby heat lamp or sun lamp (see page 17). Another touch of comfort comes from putting a towel rack next to a heat register so towels will dry quickly and be warmed.

Extending central heating

If you build an addition to house a new bathroom, you may be able to run the furnace ducts to this new room and make it a part of your central heating system. But it's advisable to check your present furnace's heating capacity and duct sizes to determine whether or not the existing heating system can handle the additional load. You might have to consider separate heating.

Supplemental heaters

If wall heaters or other supplemental heating units are used, place them so that people aren't likely to get near enough to burn themselves and so there's no possibility of towels or curtains catching fire. In general, portable heaters shouldn't be used, for safety reasons.

Any electric heaters should be safely wired with appropriate grounding to prevent electrical shock. A thermostatic control is recommended so the heater will shut off at a given temperature. If you use a gas heater, make certain it's properly vented and has a safety pilot shut-off.

A fan-assisted ceiling heater is usually adequate for blowing heat around small areas for short-term warmth.

Heated ceiling

A radiant ceiling heating system consists of gypsum wallboard with an insulated resistance wire imbedded in the core. It warms *objects* rather than the air; secondary heating occurs as air moves across the warmed objects and is heated by convection. You install this clean, noiseless system using ordinary drywall construction methods; electrical connections and thermostat installations are done by an electrician. A radiant ceiling can be painted, papered, or textured.

Providing good ventilation

Proper ventilation will help prevent such minor inconveniences as fogged mirrors and such major problems as moisture penetrating the walls. To control odor, toilet

Sill vent—*screened and slatted opening along base of projecting exterior wall—does double duty: it clears steam from lavatory mirror, airs closet through louvered door. Designer: Design Associates.*

fixtures are available with built-in venting arrangements. Ozone lamps are also effective in eliminating odors in the bathroom.

Natural ventilation

Doors and windows have until recently been the main sources of bathroom ventilation. Using them consumes no energy, but the overall room temperature changes when they're opened.

Good cross-ventilation will result from well-thought-out placement of screened windows in combination with transoms or other vents which open and close. Partial, rather than floor-to-ceiling, partitions will increase air circulation.

Fans

A ventilation fan is needed (and often required by building codes) in most bathrooms—particularly in bathrooms without windows. Fans are especially necessary in humid climates. The fan should discharge directly to the outside, either through specially built ducts or a passage that's part of a purchased fan unit. Minimum-capacity rating suggested by ventilation engineers is 12 complete air changes per hour.

Many ceiling or wall-mounted ventilation units are on the market. Most bathroom fans are one-speed, though fans with up to five speeds are available. Some fans are quieter than others; "squirrel cage" fans are generally much quieter than bladed fans. Fans come fitted with heat lamps and/or regular lamps for general room illumination. Fans can also be installed as part of a luminous ceiling.

An exhaust fan can operate on its own switch (perhaps with a timer) independently from bathroom light fixtures, or it can operate on the same switch as the light. Check local building codes regarding which electrical wiring and ventilating arrangements are approved. Some codes specify that, in a windowless bathroom, a ventilator must go on automatically when the light switch is activated.

Ways to soundproof

Walls built to provide sound control between the bathroom and adjoining rooms are a feature to consider when you're building or remodeling a bathroom; they can muffle the sounds of running water and reduce pipe noises.

The best way to control sound is to plan for it before the walls are constructed. A framing design that uses slit studs, staggered studs, or double wall studs will reduce noise. A partition system with accordion-folded gypsum wallboard between the walls also gives efficient sound control. And blanket insulation applied between the studs will lessen bathroom noise transmission through a solid wall into an adjoining room. Pipes shouldn't touch the studs or the wall surface.

The wall surfacing material (usually gypsum wallboard or plaster) should be thick. For even better soundproofing, add gypsum backer board or sound-deadening fiberboard.

Other aids to sound control include a plumbing system that has been properly sized, with pipes not isolated from the fixtures and with drainpipes slanted to slow the flow of water. In addition, you can wrap noisy pipes with several thicknesses of asphalt building paper and overwrap them with fiberglass insulation.

Other noise control measures include using a solid door and thicker glass (or even special sound control glass) and installing airtight resilient weatherstripping around doors and windows that open to the outside. Avoid undercutting a door for ventilation—such cutting aggravates any noise problem.

Unfortunately, most bathroom materials that are both easy to clean and waterproof are also hard surfaced so they reflect and echo noises. But there are exceptions: ceilings, for instance, can be constructed of materials that are both sound-absorbing and moisture resistant, and washable carpeting is a quiet flooring. Finally, you could create a pleasing auditory situation by piping sound from a radio or stereo into a bathroom with a ceiling-mounted speaker.

Fixtures & materials

- **Floorplans**
- **Lavatory basins**
- **Toilets and bidets**
- **Tubs and showers**
- **Floor, wall, ceiling, counter finishes**

The first step in designing a new or remodeled bathroom is to plan the placement, style, and color of the plumbing fixtures (basin, bathtub, shower, toilet, and bidet). They take priority because they're the most permanent design elements and may well be in use for the lifetime of the house. Then decide on a floor of tile or carpet; counter of marble, tile, plastic laminate, or wood; and papered, painted, or tiled walls that complement the fixtures.

Fixtures and materials for use in the bathroom are available in great variety. Most manufacturers offer five or more fixture colors. Select the colors of fixtures and materials with care, keeping in mind that the type of lighting you use—fluorescent, incandescent, natural—will alter the colors. Remember: specific colors change from manufacturer to manufacturer; even whites vary.

Take time to search out fixtures and materials with the special features you would most like to have in your bathroom. New design developments in bathroom fixtures and materials are occurring constantly. Dozens of special-use fixtures and materials are offered to help meet individual space and layout requirements.

Fixture placement: floor plans

The "best" bathroom floor plan doesn't exist—good plans vary according to the bathroom's size and use, its location within the house, and the number and style of fixtures to be included.

If you're remodeling an existing bath, you'll probably leave certain fixture locations undisturbed in the interest of economy. The toilet, for example, is usually best left where it is because of existing drain and vent lines, and there are obvious savings if the tub and lavatory are kept in the same general area (see the information on plumbing, pages 9-11).

However, if you're starting a new bathroom from scratch, keep an open mind about fixture placement. There are choices even where space is limited and small-scale fixtures can help you make the most of every square inch.

Minimum clearances

As a guideline, certain minimum distances between, to the side, and in front of fixtures have been established

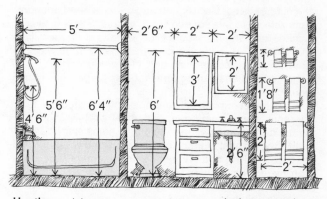

Use these *minimum measurements as a rough planning guide.*

and written into most building codes. These distances tell you how close together you can put the fixtures and still be able to use them comfortably and clean them easily. For example, if a lavatory is opposite a tub or toilet, 30 inches is a minimum clearance between them. Side-by-side fixtures, of course, can be located closer together.

Illustrated here are some examples of typical minimum clearances. Check with your local building department to find out exactly what guidelines are in effect in your community.

Basic bathroom floor plans

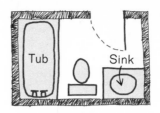

L-shaped plan, *most common design for smaller bathrooms, provides plenty of floor space, uses one wall of plumbing.*

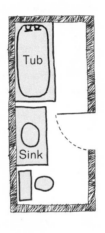

Bathroom on one wall *adapts to a long and narrow room—as narrow as 4½ feet. Here plumbing connections, drains, and vents are conveniently located along one wall.*

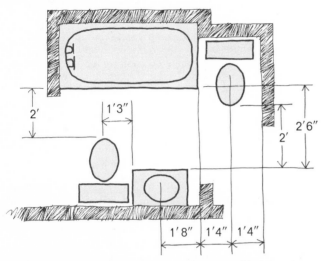

Typical minimum distances *for setting fixtures will help you in initial planning stages. But be sure to check exact local specifications before deciding on your floor plan and purchasing fixtures and materials.*

Deciding on a floor plan

Start by making cutouts to scale and, on graph paper scaled to the dimensions of your bathroom, move the fixtures around until you find the best arrangement. As you plan, be mindful of the range of fixture sizes and shapes available to you. Instead of a standard 5-foot-long bathtub, you may arrive at a better arrangement by using a 4-foot-square tub.

Position the tub before you plan the location of the other fixtures. Tub location is the first consideration simply because the tub takes up the greatest amount of space.

The basin, the most frequently used fixture, is usually best located out of the traffic zone. Because a basin with mirrors requires efficient illumination, it should be near a window to take advantage of the natural light.

If space permits, isolate the toilet with a partition or in a separate cubicle to create a sense of privacy (see compartmentalizing, page 66). In any case, the toilet should be placed where it won't be visible from the doorway. If you are planning to include a bidet, it should be positioned adjacent to the toilet.

If you want to restrict the number of walls containing plumbing pipes (this usually saves money), you'll have fewer possibilities for fixture arrangements.

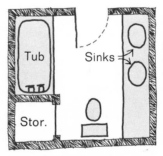

U-shaped plan *most practically utilizes space in a square room. Plumbing is more complicated, though, because it's divided and not confined to one wall.*

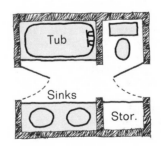

Corridor bath *can be small, could connect two bedrooms. It would be quite suitable for house with space for only one bathroom.*

What kinds of materials are best?

Smooth, easily cleaned, and nonabsorbent surfaces are most often recommended for bathrooms (and often required by codes). Check with your building department to find out if any specific materials are disallowed for bathroom use in your area.

Water causes changes in almost any material it touches. Over a period of time, any material used in a bathroom, and therefore in contact with water and moist air, will begin to change. In wood, for example, the changes range from silver gray weathering to warping, staining, and fungus growth. Stucco and concrete will streak, iron will rust, aluminum will corrode, and copper will acquire a greenish patina. These changes are not necessarily for the worse; some materials acquire a new dimension and beauty from contact with water.

Other materials, though, come close to being impervious to water; they include glass, marble, glazed tile, and laminated plastic. However, where there are joints—such as the grouting between tiles and the point at which a sheet of laminated plastic meets the tub edge—water will have an effect. But for the most part these materials will demand minimum upkeep to retain their original appearance.

Costs

Generally, materials for the bath—especially fixtures and their fittings—are priced according to quality of appearance and working performance. The more expensive ones last longer, are more attractive, and work better. And keep in mind that installation costs are the same for high or low-quality materials. Fixtures and materials that aren't standard usually cost more. Economy-type fixtures from a reputable firm will probably be well made but less attractive than higher-priced types.

Try to weigh all features of the materials you must choose from. For example, permanent-finish walls are more expensive than other wall coverings, but they require minimum maintenance; vinyl flooring is more expensive than linoleum, but it's more durable; basins with vanities cost more than wall-hung basins, but they provide greater utility and more storage space.

If you're stretching a limited budget, you'd probably be wise to buy the best fixtures you can afford as a first step, since they're relatively permanent. You can always replace floor and wall surfaces with more durable materials at a later date.

Recycled materials are often very inexpensive and can give a one-of-a-kind effect: an antique leaded glass window can be cheaper than a new window fitted with ordinary glass; old washstands, marble basins, and iron brackets are other "finds" that can be effectively adapted for modern use.

Watch, too, for sales on fixtures—sinks, tubs, and toilets—as well as on the other materials you will be using.

Fixture materials

Most standard plumbing fixtures are made from any one of five materials: porcelain-enameled stamped steel, porcelain-enameled cast iron, stainless steel, vitreous china, and fiberglass-reinforced plastic. Each has its own particular advantages and disadvantages; your choice will be influenced by your budget and the scope of your bathroom project.

Enameled cast-iron fixtures are about three times heavier than enameled steel fixtures, making them more costly to ship and handle. And wrestling their heavy, awkward forms into a house can be difficult. But cast-iron fixtures—the world's standard since 1890—are durable, retain their glossy finish for years, and come in a variety of shapes. Bathtubs and basins made of this material resist chipping and keep water hot for a long time.

Enameled steel incorporates a special blend of metals used for manufacturing strong but lightweight products. It isn't as durable as enameled cast iron because it has a thinner coat of enamel, but it is much lighter weight. Enameled steel fixtures are often used for remodeling because they're comparatively easy to carry to the site. They come in a pleasing array of colors and can last indefinitely if the surface is cleaned with nonabrasive products.

Stainless steel for bathroom use appears mainly in basins. This durable material reportedly will never discolor and is usually unaffected by household chemicals. Stainless steel fixtures are generally sound deadened. Hard water will spot stainless steel, and soap residue shows up more on stainless steel than on porcelain enamel. Though these stains are easily removed, stainless steel fixtures do require more frequent cleaning than others to keep a spotless look.

Vitreous china is a carefully balanced mixture of clays that is poured into molds and dried. The resulting shape is sprayed with a glaze and fired in kilns. This attractive, easy-to-clean material is used for most toilets and bidets, and for many types of basins.

Fiberglass-reinforced plastic is molded at the factory into seamless, lightweight fixtures that can be installed quickly and easily. Colorful tubs and basins in new and different shapes and one-piece tub and shower combinations are commonly made of this material. They often have built-in extra features such as grab bars, shower seats, arm rests, and soap niches. Fiberglass-reinforced plastic is warmer to the touch than steel or iron. However, it requires extra maintenance to retain its initial sparkle.

Lavatory basins

Beautifully carved marble, gleaming metal, exotic giant clam shells, handcrafted pottery—any of these can be a delightful basin as long as it's the right shape and waterproof. Check unusual basins with local building authorities first, though.

Commercial lavatories, sinks, or washbasins (as they're variously called) come in shapes and sizes to suit almost any building or remodeling plan. Shapes include rectangular, square, oval, round, triangular, and D-shapes; sizes as widely varying as 11 by 11 inches,

19 by 16 inches, and 30 by 20 inches are available. To further visualize the wide range of styles from which you can choose, consider just the back of the basin: you can obtain basins with a shelf ledge, a slant, plain, or flat back. A range of bright colors further widens the choice, and to fit different decorative schemes there's a variety of designs, ranging from a simple Greek key trim to all-over floral patterns.

Space-saving *corner basin hangs on wall. Some types come with a splashback.*

Placement of the fittings (faucets) varies with the type of basin you select, but you have two basic options: to put the fittings directly on the basin or to install them in the counter, apart from the basin. (For more information on fittings, see pages 55-56.)

Standard height from the floor to the basin rim is 31 to 34 inches; you can have the basin placed higher or lower to suit your height and preference. An 8-inch space between the top of the lavatory and the bottom of a mirror or medicine cabinet installed above it is recommended. On countertops with an integral splashback, it's logical to position the mirror at the top of the splash.

Examine the actual lavatories available from the manufacturers before you make a final choice. Newer features include shampoo spray attachments, lotion dispensers, and swing-away spouts.

Wall-hung basins

This type of sink may be supported entirely by the bathroom wall, or it may have additional support from a pedestal or legs. Cabinets for storage can be built

Supported *mainly by wall hangers, basin also rests on graceful pedestal.*

under it, but the main support for the basin still comes from wall brackets or hangers. Most wall-hung lavatories are rectangular. Basins that fit into a corner can save space in a small bathroom.

In replacing one wall-hung sink with another, you'll want to replace the old bracket with a new one. If you're installing a wall-hung sink for the first time, you'll have to tear out that part of the wall directly behind the sink.

Countertop basins

Most basins are made to be supported by a counter, often with a cabinet structure underneath. (For cabinet ideas, see the section about storage on pages 51-53.) Prefabricated units complete with cabinet, counter, and integral basin are available. Whatever counter or cabinet structure you choose, be sure to leave sufficient space around the pipes to permit repairs. (For more information on counters, see page 31.)

Four countertop basins

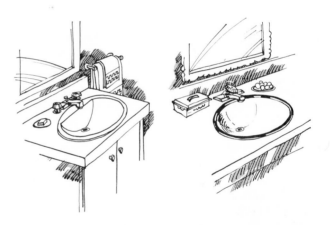

Surface-mounted   **Flush-mounted**

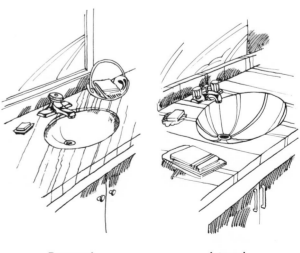

Recessed   **Integral**

Styles. Countertop sinks may be rectangular, square, oval, or round. Usually they're either self-rimming with an integral lip that overlaps the counter opening to form a water seal (surface-mount), or they're recessed with a surrounding metal rim which provides the seal (flush-mount). Flush-mount sinks require precise fitting for a watertight seal. Incidentally, the metal rims can be found in finishes to match your hardware, so don't settle for a chrome rim if you have brass or gold-plated fittings.

Two other types of countertop sinks are available. One type fits underneath the countertop, so the edge of the counter overlaps the basin. The under-the-counter basin can be difficult to keep clean; it works best with a smooth counter of marble, synthetic marble, or sheet plastic. Also available are sinks that are integral with the counter. These one-piece sink and counter units are the easiest type to clean. With both the under-counter and integral sinks, fittings are mounted through the countertop instead of on the basin rim.

Double basins. Countertop lavatories are ideal where two basins are needed, since the basins can be joined by a continuous surface. A minimum of 12 inches should be provided between adjoining basin edges. Better yet is a 20-inch space for more elbow room when two people use double basins. The basin should be no closer than 6 to 8 inches from the side edge of the counter to provide a small ledge and to prevent splashing on the floor. Locating basins at extreme ends of an L-shaped counter is one method of providing ample elbow room. A special hair-washing sink with a spray attachment might serve as the second basin.

Choosing a toilet

Toilets (called "water closets" in building circles) vary in style, size, shape, installation, and mechanism. New colors brighten the selection, and toilets are more attractively designed and lower than they used to be.

In planning toilet placement, allow one inch between the toilet tank and the wall behind it, 15 inches to the center of the bowl from the side wall, and not less than 18 inches from the facing wall. If a toilet must face the door, allow room for the door to swing all the way open.

Replacing a noisy, old toilet with a newer model is relatively simple. Most floor-mounted toilets are designed to attach to standard fittings for water and waste piping, and though the installation procedure involves working with heavy, bulky objects in cramped space, it doesn't demand great plumbing skill.

Differences in flushing mechanism

Toilets commonly used for residences have a variety of flushing actions. These different actions result from bowl design and vary in noise generated, efficiency, and price.

Washdown toilets are the least expensive, least efficient, and most noisy. This type is most easily recognized by a characteristic bulge on the front exterior. It has a very small water surface inside the bowl, with a large, flat, exposed china surface at the front of the bowl interior. Since this area isn't protected by water, it's subject to staining and is difficult to clean. The washdown bowl is no longer accepted by many municipal code authorities.

Reverse trap action is efficient but moderately noisy. More of the interior surface is covered by water than in the washdown type.

Siphon jet is an improved version of the reverse trap— quieter and more efficient but also more expensive. Most of the exposed china surface is covered by water.

Siphon action mechanism is a refinement of the siphon jet. The toilet is a one-piece unit that's almost silent as it operates, leaves no dry surfaces, and is efficient and attractive. It's the most expensive.

Up-flush toilets are used in basements when the sewer is above basement floor level. They need no pipes below the basement floor. Instead, water enters through a double-acting flush valve. You purchase everything from the water-supply pipe to the sewage riser pipe as a package with the fixture; full plumbing and installation instructions come with the toilet.

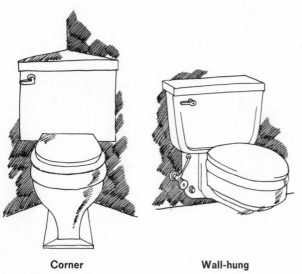

Three types of toilets

Some styles are quieter and easier to clean; most models are available in a wide variety of colors.

Corner   Wall-hung   Siphon jet

What styles are available?

In addition to differences in flushing mechanism, toilets have other features to choose from.

Wall-hung toilets. A good-looking, though expensive, alternative to the standard floor-mounted toilet is the wall-hung type. It makes floor cleaning easy. Unlike floor-mounted types, it won't drip from tank condensation. A wall-hung unit, however, must have a rather circuitous drainage layout, and it clogs more easily than floor-mounted toilets.

Installation of a wall-hung toilet calls for extensive modification of existing piping and alteration of the bathroom wall. This toilet requires a 6-inch wall for support (instead of the usual 4-inch wall), sometimes reinforced by a heavy L-brace that attaches to the floor. Since it expels waste through a wall connection, it requires the shifting of an existing soil pipe from its usual opening in the floor.

A special type of wall-hung toilet, the lever-flushed model, is usually confined to commercial installations because it requires strong water pressure and is expensive to install, but since it has no working parts, it's easier to maintain.

Water-saver toilets. Some toilet models are designed to make effective use of a low volume of water; they often utilize one-third less water than other toilets per use. Water-saver types may be hard to find in some areas, but they're becoming more commonplace. A typical low-volume standard toilet requires only 3 gallons of water rather than the usual 5 to 7-gallon gulp. New state and federal energy conservation standards may specify a maximum 3-gallon-per-flush water use.

Corner toilets. These toilets save space and are especially valuable in tiny half-baths. The tanks are triangular to fit precisely into a corner.

Elongated bowl toilets. Also called "extended rim toilets," these models are very attractive and easier to clean than round bowl designs. The extra inches create more comfortable seating and more water surface area. Municipal codes have required elongated bowls in commercial locations for many years. Now some cities are extending the requirement to apartment buildings.

Higher seat toilets. This type of toilet proves particularly useful for the aged or infirm. The rim of the bowl is 18 inches above the floor, in contrast to the 14-inch height of conventional bowls.

Accessories and options. If you foresee a problem with a sweating toilet tank, you can either purchase an internal drip guard or use an insulated tank. Devices are available that bring the water up to room temperature to prevent condensation—these either plug into an electric outlet or are installed beneath the tank. Some toilet models come with venting devices built into the flush mechanism.

Other extra touches are tank lids with integral planters, push-buttons instead of handles, and furniture-like frames that fit around standard toilets to make them look like chairs.

Lids, lid covers, and seats come in many materials, colors, and designs. Many of these lift off easily for cleaning.

A toilet paper holder may be decorative or merely functional, but it must be conveniently placed. The center of the toilet paper roll should be 26 inches from the floor; the edge of the roll should be 6 inches forward from the front of the bowl.

A magazine or book rack is another accessory to consider for the toilet area.

Bidets

If your bathroom has open floor area that could accommodate an additional fixture, consider installing a bidet. Used primarily for washing the perineal area, it is a sit-down wash basin provided with both hot and cold water and often a spray.

The usual location for a bidet is alongside the toilet. A bidet requires a minimum 3 by 3-foot floor area next to a wall. Installation can be quite expensive because of the need for both hot and cold-water connections and for a suitable drain. Fitting plumbing for a bidet into the existing piping involves opening walls and flooring.

Bidets come in colors to match the other fixtures. They're slightly lower than toilets in height.

Similar in design *to a sitz bath or a footbath, a bidet can substitute for them.*

Types of bathtubs

Many people feel that a luxurious bathtub is the item to splurge on when they plan a bathroom. Consequently, custom tubs of marble, tile, and wood are very popular. If you use reinforced concrete or fiberglass for a tub structure, almost any shape can be created.

But if you're on a budget, you'll be pleased to find that manufactured tubs are available in a widening range of sizes, colors, and shapes designed to meet specific requirements.

The substitution of a more modern tub for an old one can easily qualify as major home surgery rather than simple home improvement. This tends to be a big project for the weekend plumber because the task calls for know-how—and a clear track from the unloading site to the bathroom so that you can maneuver a heavy tub around corners, through doorways, and down hallways. Going up stairs is quite an undertaking.

To remove a built-in bathtub, you'll have to tear out the walls that enclose it. An enameled steel tub has a flange running along the sides to be fitted into a wall. Since a cast-iron tub has no flange, braces are needed between the studs.

To save on installation costs, choose a tub that will fit into the same space as the one it's replacing. Shorter, longer, and wider tubs often require changes in the house framing.

For information on tub and shower curtains and doors, see pages 56-57.

What kinds are available?

The most common tub, a rectangle 5 feet long by 30 inches wide, contributed to the predominance of 5-by-8-foot bathrooms. But new, more comfortable tub sizes are available, and new tub shapes and colors.

See page 22 for information about the materials tubs are made from. Typically, a standard tub made from enameled cast iron weighs from 350 to 500 pounds, an enameled steel tub weighs 100 to 250 pounds, and a fiberglass tub weighs 60 to 70 pounds.

Some bathtubs are designed with the drain in the angle formed by the end wall and floor rather than entirely on the floor of the tub. This type of fixture can be attached to drainpipes which run above the floor, as in concrete slab floor construction.

Standard rectangular tubs most often measure 5 feet long, 29 to 32 inches wide, and 16 inches high. This type of tub is readily available at most plumbing shops. Tubs in 4, 4½, 5½ and 6-foot lengths are generally available on special order. Some rectangular tubs have an oval-shaped or angled depression that provides the additional benefit of a built-in ledge for shampoo and soap. Larger rectangular tubs sometimes have a built-in seat on one side.

Most plumbing fixture makers offer standard rectangular tubs that can be installed flush with one, two, or three walls of the bathroom. The sides of the tub to be joined with walls have flanges which speed installation of finished wall materials and help prevent moisture from getting into the framing.

Modular tub/showers can replace both the tub and its enclosure. Often cast in one piece of fiberglass, these units are also available in a special kit for remodelers—this version comes in four pieces, neatly enclosed in two manageable cartons. For more information about showers, see pages 27-28.

Receptor tubs are low, squarish units, excellent for bathing children and doubling as the shower base for adults. Typical receptor tubs are 31 to 48 inches long, 42 to 49 inches wide, and 12 to 16 inches high. They can be set in a corner or recessed in a small alcove.

Square tubs fit nicely into corners. Some have seating niches at the corners. These range in size from a small 4-by-4-foot model to a capacious 5 by 5 feet. Square tubs have some disadvantages: they're difficult for elderly people to get into and out of, they demand a large volume of water, and they're awkward to clean.

Having high sides, this receptor (base) for a shower can serve as small bathtub. Receptor tubs usually have a corner seat, as do most square tubs.

Sunken tubs give an elegant effect. Standard sunken tubs come in varying shapes, sizes, and depths. Check the capacity of your water heater if you're planning a sunken tub of larger-than-normal size.

A sunken tub can be installed as part of a remodeling project if there's room under the floor to accommodate it. This space may be provided by the crawl area beneath the first floor, a garage under a second-story bathroom, or even a stairwell. Extra framing is often necessary to carry the weight of a sunken tub built on the second story.

Before installing a sunken tub, consider the safety hazards involved. Sunken tubs can cause accidents in households with small children or elderly residents. The potential hazard can usually be reduced by careful design which treats the sunken tub as a separate entity, like a miniature indoor swimming pool. Handy grab bars are highly desirable.

Oversize tubs large enough to hold two adults are also available from your plumbing supply dealer. These require substantial support framing and a back-up water heater, and you should make sure the one you want can be brought into your house through existing doorways.

Built-in recessed inlets direct swirling water into whirlpool tub; portable whirlpool units are also available.

Whirlpool tubs with built-in hydromassage units are costly because of the jet-pump mechanism and the extensive changes in piping and wiring needed for their installation. But for those who enjoy this exhilarating type of tub bath, the extra expense may be worth it. These tubs are available in various materials in square and rectangular shapes, sunken and oversize models.

Japanese tubs (furos) are available in fiberglass and, in some areas, traditional wood. This tub is a deep well that accommodates one or more soakers seated in steaming water up to the chin. Such a tub may require space under the floor to accommodate the extra depth and is probably best installed at ground level. It also may need an extra-capacity water heater or a supplementary heater of its own. (See pages 74-75.)

Safety and convenience features

Check for nonslip texture in the bottom surface of any tub that you wish to purchase. Texturing is particularly desirable if the tub is to be used as a shower also. Some new models have a mildly roughened surface that's too subtle to emboss the anatomy of a person sitting in the tub, yet rough enough to discourage a foot from skidding. This style has replaced the patterned tub bottoms popular a few years ago, which have proved difficult to keep clean and less skid-resistant than originally thought. (Avoid the temptation to add stick-on skid pads in the tub. These wear off in time, provide little actual skid resistance, and offer a refuge for dirt and bacteria.)

Tubs with built-in lumbar supports are more comfortable than those with all sides vertical. Headrests and armrests are also available. Grab bars built into the sides of tubs are becoming more common, especially on large rectangular tubs. Though drains are usually placed under the faucets, you can get tubs with drains positioned elsewhere. A drain at the opposite end of the tub from the faucets makes tub cleaning easier.

You can determine the water depth of a bathtub by measuring the distance from the overflow to the bottom drain. A foot of water in the tub is needed for a good soaking.

Around the tub you'll need places for sponges, soap, shampoo, bath oils, and brushes; a rack to hang towels and washcloths; and a spot to store towels.

Showers and tub/showers

Shower stalls can be fabricated during construction of a new bathroom, or they can be purchased in prefabricated form—various manufacturers produce them. A shower can be in combination with a bathtub, in a separate stall or compartment, or in a portion of the bathroom that has undergone waterproofing and drain installation for use as a doorless shower area. For information on outside showers, see pages 72-73. Ideas on types of shower fittings are on pages 55-56.

Showers can be purchased or constructed in a variety of sizes, but for comfort, a shower stall should be at least 3 feet square.

The most economical way to provide a shower is to add a shower head to an existing bathtub. The two ways to convert a tub to a tub/shower are to build a spray head into the wall above the tub or to add a movable spray head on a flexible cable. If permanent shower fittings are installed, the pipes for the shower are usually concealed in the wall. A movable shower head can be added without changing the plumbing; it's likely to use less water than a regular shower, and it's useful for cleaning the tub.

Shower and tub/shower enclosure materials

The wall surfaces around any type of shower must be finished in a moisture-resistant material. Plastic laminates, ceramic tile, cultured marble, and fiberglass-reinforced plastic are some of the materials that can be used.

Tiled, sunken tub/shower *has convex skylight that allows standup head room. Architect: Ed Heine.*

It's important that this wall surface be installed properly because considerable damage can result if the joints aren't water resistant.

Some manufacturers of bathtub and shower combinations solve the watertight installation problem by making shower walls of fiberglass-reinforced plastic integral with a fiberglass shower base or tub. The entire unit is installed as one fixture.

Other tub/shower surrounds are made in three sections that fit around the top of the bathtub. The sheets are sealed to each other and to the top of the tub so that water can't leak through to the wall. Laminated hardboard or melamine-laminated plywood panels designed expressly as tub enclosures can be attached directly to the studs or applied over gypsum wallboard. Most cities require that gypsum wallboard behind a tub or shower be a special water-resistant type.

Manufactured showers

Standard showers are constructed of fiberglass-reinforced plastic or of metal.

Lightweight molded fiberglass showers and tub/showers have a smooth surface with rounded corners for easy cleaning and can be quickly set in place and attached to framing members. The shower stalls are available in two styles. One is a complete stall—floor, three walls, and optional ceiling—molded as a single, large unit. The other, designed for remodeling projects, is formed of four basic components that are glued together on the site. The drain mechanism is usually part of the package. Fiberglass units come in a choice of colors; sizes and heights vary. They often have soap dishes, ledges, towel racks, and seats molded into the structure during manufacture.

Integral *tub/shower and wall surround made of seamless fiberglass can come with molded-in soap dishes, ledges, niches, or a seat.*

However, there are some possible problems. If a combination shower and shower enclosure comes in one piece—especially if it's a tub/shower—the unit might not pass through narrow hallways or through the bathroom door. Fiberglass will scratch if you clean it with abrasive cleaners. Precisely tailored framing is required to give fiberglass units firm surrounding support and to make sure that their rectangular box form will fit into an irregular space without flexing when in use.

If a fiberglass unit appeals to you, shop for it carefully. Some of the first-generation models were flimsy, and a few may still be on the market. Arrange with the plumbing supply dealer to show you the latest models in his warehouse or stock room. Examine construction features carefully before investing. A high-quality product, made by a reputable firm and properly installed, will give trouble-free service indefinitely. The latest models are more resistant to scuffing and chemical stains (except nicotine) than some of the earlier ones. The fiberglass is coated with a protective gel sealant that wears off in time. You can postpone this dulling by cleaning with liquid cleansers instead of abrasive powders. The original surface can be restored by the company that installs the fiberglass unit.

Metal showers are also available. Tin is very inexpensive but extremely noisy, and tin shower stalls vibrate. Cheaper metals can rust. Stainless steel showers are more expensive and attractive, but they water spot.

Custom showers

Custom showers are generally more expensive than standard ones, but in some cases they're the only kind that will fit into the bathroom design the homeowner has in mind. Ceramic tile is used for most custom showers, but other waterproof surfacing materials can be used. Careful attention must be given to waterproofing joints.

Tiled showers are relatively expensive and the joints can be difficult to clean, but silicone grouts are said to discourage mildew growth. Tile can be applied with mastic over gypsum wallboard or plaster, or it can be set into wet mortar. Pregrouted tile shower surrounds are available in sizes to fit the most popular receptors. They consist of several pregrouted sheets and internal corner strips. Limited on-site grouting and cuts are required.

The floor of a custom shower is usually either a purchased waterproof receptor, available in a range of colors, types, and sizes, or a fabricated receptor of ceramic tile or some other suitable material. The standard prefabricated receptors come in set dimensions. A custom-built shower base requires the installation of a shower pan made of sheet lead or copper or a waterproof and damp-proof membrane formed to the desired size and shape. The membrane, frequently a lamination of heavy paper and asphalt reinforced with glass fibers, costs considerably less than sheet lead or copper.

When planning a custom shower, consult a contractor or plumber to make sure that construction will conform with local building and sanitation codes.

Accessories for safety, convenience

Look into a number of ways to make your shower safer. To prevent falls, install a vertical grab bar, making sure screws attach it through the wall into the studs. Make certain the shower door (see page 56) operates easily and won't break. Any light fixture used above a shower should be vaporproof. An exhaust fan will aid in removing moisture and vapor. The base of the shower should have a nonskid surface.

Thermal mixing valves make it easier to get the desired water temperature. Other fixtures allow you to dial the temperature you want. (See pages 55-56 for more information on shower fittings and accessories.)

The shower head should be installed high enough to ensure head clearance for adults. A storage shelf approximately 40 inches above the shower floor is convenient. All shower surfaces, including any seat or shelf, should be self draining.

The choice in floor finishes

Since bathroom floors are subjected to water and moisture, they should be surfaced with materials that resist water. Resilient flooring (in tile or sheet form), carpeting, and ceramic tile are the most commonly used flooring materials in bathrooms. Other possibilities include polyurethaned stenciled, painted, or natural wood, poured floors, or marble floors. Wood floors may need to be refinished periodically with a water-resistant seal or varnish. Rugs are often used in bathrooms as accents. To make concrete floors more attractive, consider adding color to the cement mixture at the time of construction or painting the finished floor with one of the special concrete floor paints.

No one floor finish has all the properties desirable in a bathroom floor. The flooring decision may depend on your skill in installation if you plan to do the job yourself. Many of the troubles that develop with bathroom floor finishes can be attributed to poor installation. Other considerations include durability of the floor finish, its cost, ease of upkeep, resistance to soil and indentation, and quietness.

Light or neutral flooring colors offer the most flexibility in decorating and make small bathrooms appear larger than dark or patterned floors do. Select materials in colors that you won't tire of quickly.

How to carpet
a bathroom

Repair the floor if it's worn (especially if it has wide cracks or depressions) and remove the bathroom door. Be careful not to disturb plumbing connections. Make a pattern from heavy paper, as shown in photo sequence. Spread carpeting, face down, on a bare floor. Piece as necessary and lay pattern *also face down* on carpeting. If possible, position the pattern so a bound edge of carpeting will fall along the door sill. Tape pattern to carpeting. When you can, cut between rows of tufting to avoid cutting the stitches.

You'll need *squares of heavy paper, cellophane tape, masking tape, and scissors; possibly a pencil, measuring tape, and razor blades.*

Starting in corner, *make pattern of floor by taping squares of heavy paper together, letting them overlap each other by ½ inch.*

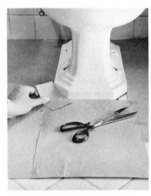

Keeping edges snug, *fit pattern around fixtures and indentations for door jamb molding. Cover floor; leave slit from back of each fixture to the wall. Remove pattern.*

Place pattern face down *on the back of the carpet and tape it to carpet securely. Cut slits for fixtures as the pattern indicates; then cut out the openings for the fixtures.*

Seam carpet *by laying sections side by side, taping them together with masking tape or a pressure sensitive tape. You'll have to repeat the process after each laundering.*

Finished carpet *is soft and warm underfoot. The heavier the carpet, the smoother it will be. Because of splashing in children's baths, avoid carpeting unless floor is heated.*

Carpeting in a bathroom

Carpeting under bare feet is great on cold winter mornings. Besides contributing warmth, carpeting can prevent slips and falls; and a bottle or glass dropped on a carpeted floor will probably bounce rather than break. Soft carpeting is quieter than hard flooring materials.

It's advisable to use washable carpeting, such as nylon, loose laid so it can be removed periodically for cleaning. Some synthetic fibers retard water absorption; some carpeting is treated with mildew, stain, and odor-resistant substances. Tweeds and patterns don't show soil as fast as solid colors.

If you anticipate needing extra resistance to stain and wear, kitchen carpeting is a practical choice. Indoor-outdoor carpeting is another durable possibility, though it tends to retain water. Inexpensive carpeting is available at special remnant sales and at overrun outlets.

Some backing materials, such as vinyl foam, stand up well to moisture. Carpeting with a backing is more comfortable to stand on, especially for a first-floor bathroom on a concrete slab.

Even though you intend to install carpeting, the floor underneath should be in good condition; otherwise, moisture soaking through the carpeting may cause permanent damage to the floor support structure. Worn floors may be hidden successfully by carpeting, but they shouldn't be worn to such an extent that they no longer protect the subflooring.

Using ceramic tile

Matte or crystalline glazed ceramic tile is more durable than highly glazed wall tile, which is usually not used on the floor. (But there are always exceptions: the beauty of highly glazed tile may outweigh more practical considerations.) Unglazed mosaic tile makes a very durable floor, as does quarry tile. Shapes of floor tiles include hexagons, octagons, rectangles, large or small squares, and Spanish or Moorish patterns. Tile surfaces can be smooth, abrasive nonslip, or carved.

Tiles of hardened impervious glass are also available in a broad range of shapes and colors for use on floors or walls. Cement grout is suggested for glass tiles.

Most tile companies manufacture floor tile which harmonizes with the colors of their wall tile. If you want a blend of tile colors, you can order different percentages of each shade. Varying tile textures, shapes, and colors can be combined for individual effects. Tile manufacturers often stock a selection of popular blends and multicolor patterns.

Colored grout can be used as a design element. When contrasting grout is used, special precautions must be taken to seal the tile before the grout is applied.

Floor tiles can be installed over concrete, plywood, wood, or hardboard, at grade or above grade level. Pregrouted sheets of tile save installation time. Smooth-surfaced polyurethane grout resists stains, mildew, bacteria, and chemical corrosion, and it's flexible enough to move as the house structure settles. Because water eventually seeps through the grout (though it won't penetrate the tiles themselves) the backing must be durable and not affected by water.

Be sure to purchase and save extra tiles for possible future repairs and replacements. Patterns and glazes change, and often it's impossible to match colors a few years after the initial installation.

Resilient flooring

These floorings—linoleum, vinyl, vinyl asbestos, asphalt, rubber, and cork—come in either sheet or tile form. Sheet materials are less susceptible to moisture leaking through because they're installed with a minimum of seams (sheets are available in rolls up to 12 feet wide); tiles are easier to work with than sheet floorings, and tiles of different colors and styles can be combined for special effects. Tiles are intended to be cemented in place to serve as a permanent floor. Sheet materials are also usually cemented but in some cases can be left loose like rugs. Whichever type of resilient flooring you use, a waterproof adhesive or moisture-resistant backing will help protect against water damage. The floor to be covered must be in good condition—smooth, dry, firm, and free from grease, wax, and oil.

Resilient tiles generally come in 12-inch squares in many colors and patterns. Some have an embossed surface texture. Self-stick tiles even have the adhesive already applied to the tiles. Of the resilient tile floorings, asphalt is the least expensive; it costs approximately one-third of the installed price of rubber or vinyl tile. Asphalt tile is very durable but is more susceptible to staining than linoleum. Vinyl asbestos tile has a coating

of clear plastic that wears well. This material is priced between asphalt and vinyl tile.

Some resilient flooring materials, including linoleum and cork, cannot be used on grade or below grade in a basement bathroom; others, such as asphalt, rubber, solid vinyl, and vinyl asbestos, can. Be sure to get the type of flooring and adhesive recommended.

Deluxe resilient floorings come with permanent no-wax finishes; cushioned floorings offer extra comfort and quiet.

Finishes for the walls and ceiling

Many of the same materials are used on both bathroom walls and ceilings. A few materials, such as acoustical tile, are usually confined to ceiling use. The ceiling should be completed before the walls are decorated. Walls around showers and tubs must meet specific moisture-resistance requirements (see page 27).

The other bathroom walls should be reasonably protected from moisture damage. This protection is more critical in small, enclosed bathrooms where humidity builds up quickly than in larger, more open bathrooms. Check local codes for any restrictions on the type of bathroom wall finish you can use. Water-resistant wall materials include ceramic tile, mirrors, vinyl products, plastic-finished or laminated hardboards, and marble. Other wall materials used in bathrooms include wood with protective finishes, painted plaster or gypsum wallboard, and vinyl-protected wallcoverings.

The color, pattern, and texture of the wall surface has a strong effect on the overall color scheme and decorative effect of a bathroom since the walls make up a large percentage of the room area. A prominent pattern on the walls will overshadow the other features of the bathroom; choose accessories accordingly to avoid a clash of patterns or styles. If you can't find a wall finish to match the fixture colors exactly, it's better to use contrasting colors on the walls.

Using wallpapers and fabrics

Wallpapers, fabrics, and vinyl wallcoverings come in many colors and designs. They're often available with matching fabrics that you can use for curtains or a shower curtain.

Vinyl-laminated, vinyl-coated and plastic-coated wallpapers are washable and scrubbable and will stand up well under humidity. Vinyl-coated fabric is also available in many different patterns and colors. You could apply a waterproofer over standard fabric or paper.

Wallpapering a small bathroom is relatively inexpensive. If the room is large, try papering one wall.

Prepasted and pretrimmed papers make it easier to do the work yourself; strippable papers make changes easier. Check to be sure that the adhesive is moisture-proof.

Paint in the bathroom

Paint is an inexpensive, easy-to-apply bathroom wall finish. Paint used on bathroom walls should be moisture

and mildew resistant and easy to clean. Alkyds (oil-based) paints should be used on bath walls and ceilings—these paints are both durable and washable. The higher the gloss, the smoother the finish and, consequently, the easier it is to clean. Gloss or semi-gloss enamel is commonly recommended for bathrooms.

Paint can be custom mixed to match fixtures and other items exactly.

Ceramic and plastic tile for walls

Ceramic tiles have traditionally been the first choice for bathroom walls. Wall tiles vary from 1-by-1-inch squares to huge Spanish shapes measuring 9½ inches from tip to tip. The most frequently used wall tile measures 4½ by 4½ inches. Wall tiles often have a bright, shiny glaze. When decorated tile is used, it becomes a very important design element.

For more information on using ceramic tile, see page 30.

Plastic wall tile is inexpensive and comparatively easy for a home workman to install. Like ceramic tile, plastic tile is available in many colors.

Rigid wall panels

Most wall panels can be installed quickly and easily; just be sure they'll fit through the doorway. The expanding range of paneling colors and patterns makes for interesting decorating possibilities.

Sheet vinyl for bathroom use comes with a moisture-resistant backing; some brands of plastic laminates, familiar as counter coverings, are available also for use on bathroom walls. Some plastic laminate panels have a polystyrene core that compensates for subwall irregularities. Plastic-coated hardboards wipe clean easily.

Decking (above) salvaged from old ship covers shower walls; tiles line tub base. Outside entrance lets swimmers in to share double-size tub/shower without crossing carpet.
Etched porthole (right) near shower displays walrus.

Ship's linen closet converts to bath vanity. Marble facing from razed building covers top of counter.

Counter possibilities

Counters next to a sink should be water resistant; they needn't be waterproof if you wipe off splashes right away. But check your local codes to see if they restrict counter materials.

The range of materials that can be used as counter-tops is wide. Counters can be made of the same material as the walls or the floor. If there's cabinetry under the counter, the color and type of counter material should coordinate with the color, material, and style of the cabinets (see pages 51-53). Counters containing an integral sink are available in several materials, such as laminated plastic and simulated marble, in a choice of sizes and shapes.

Ceramic tile, plastic laminate, and plastic-coated hardboard are the most common bathroom counter materials. Simulated marble is also very popular. With tile, initial installation is expensive, but tile is more durable than most other surfaces. Plastic laminate is easy to clean and inexpensive to install. Counters can also be made of polyurethaned wood, metal, or marble (listed from least to most expensive).

Bathroom ideas in color

- **Bathrooms before and after**

- **Stained glass; wall materials**

- **Basins and mirrors**

- **Bedroom-bath combinations**

- **Garden baths**

- **Bathtubs, showers, saunas**

The following pages offer an array of bathrooms. In each one, the various design elements—such as floor plan, textures, colors, and illumination—have been used differently to suit different tastes.

But these bathrooms all have one thing in common: each is a well-thought-out whole. All the design elements in each bathroom create a unified effect.

It's probably neither possible nor wise for you to reproduce exactly one of the bathrooms shown here. Look at them for ideas. Consider every element shown, evaluating it in relation to your own needs and taste.

For example, almost every bathroom shown uses plants for atmosphere and color. On the facing page, plants spill out of a built-in, high-up planter; in the bathroom at the bottom of page 36, layers of glass shelves hold green plants that frame a mirror. These are among the ideas you might adapt for your own bathroom.

Allow for coordinating bathroom decoration into the already-established scheme for the rest of the house.

The first part of this chapter (pages 33 to 39) illustrates and describes examples of inadequate bathrooms that have been improved by remodeling and redecorating. In most cases the owners saved money by doing part of the work themselves—in some instances they did all the work. Studying these examples may help you discover new potential in your present bathroom.

If you want a change from a small, enclosed bathroom, you might consider opening your new one to a bedroom or to the out-of-doors. See pages 44 and 45 for ways that other people have done this.

On pages 40 and 41 are bathrooms that illustrate a variety of specific methods of introducing color and texture. Multicolored stained glass in different styles and colors—both new and recycled examples—has been used for completely different effects in four bathrooms. In two other bathrooms, it's the wall material that makes the color and texture statement.

Basins (pages 42-43), tubs (pages 46-47), and showers and saunas (page 48) are all important elements in a bathroom—a special one can be the focal point around which a bathroom is designed. Our examples show custom, out-of-the-ordinary fixtures.

Before: *Extremely small and cramped, bathroom was outdated and inconvenient.*

BATHROOMS BEFORE
...AND AFTER

More storage *surrounds the toilet; shelf hinges up for access to tank. Built-in, metal-lined planter holds potted plants that thrive under the high-up skylight. Neat triangular shelves add convenience to tub/shower.*

Corner basin *saves space; long edge of counter visually enlarges room. Floor, counter, and tub are tiled; wood trim is mostly red oak with some maple. Wood rungs of towel ladder were recessed in the studs.*

Storage fits everywhere in small bath

Here the most pressing problem was the lack of ventilation and natural light. A room added on in a previous remodeling project had rendered useless the existing small window.

Minor structural modifications totally changed the bathroom. The useless window was covered over; an opening up through the attic allowed installation of a high, dramatic skylight that brings in light and creates a feeling of vertical space.

The owners did the painting themselves and contracted the rest of the work.

Architect: Michael D. Moyer.

Specially shaped drawers *fit into triangular cabinet. Scale-in-a-drawer pulls out at the tug of a toe.*

BATHROOMS BEFORE ...AND AFTER

Before: *Typical of its era, the 7½ by 10-foot, 1936 bath had only one place in which to put things—a wall-hung medicine cabinet.*

Owner-built *new oak units provide storage both on the wall and below the sinks; two sinks provide multiple use for a family of three.*

Now the side yard enhances bathroom

This remodeled bathroom takes advantage of a narrow side yard instead of hiding it as before. Vines traveling up fishline outside the windows and the pale amber glass combine to ensure privacy.

The standard tub, sheathed with wood, incorporates an open planter box at one end to hold potted plants. Architect: Mark Mills.

Redesigned, rebuilt by the owners

The range of light and dark tones in the wood used for walls and cabinets adds surface interest. Dark grout contrasts with large white tile squares on the counter and the splashback. White-painted, rough-feeling adobe tub walls introduce another natural texture.

This bathroom exchanged space with the adjoining kitchen. The kitchen now is larger; the bathroom is still a comfortable size and efficient.

The owners did the plumbing, wiring, and tile work themselves.

Plans: *Sink was moved and set in an alcove, and bathroom entrance was moved. Soil stack stayed in same place.*

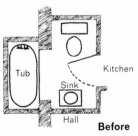

Before

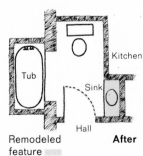

Remodeled feature ▨

After

Soffit light *over basin supplements ceiling fixtures. Wooden towel racks and paper holder were designed, built by the owner.*

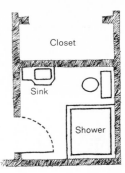

Closet

Sink

Shower

Before

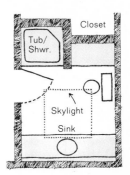

Tub/ Shwr.

Closet

Skylight

Sink

After

Remodeled feature

Plans: *To expand and modernize bathroom, adjacent bedroom closet was added.*

Twin arches *that blend with the architecture of the rest of the house fill one wall. Adjustable glass shelves in the second arch allow light to reach plants.*

Handy, pull-out cabinet *has two plastic bin inserts: one is used as a laundry hamper, the other as a waste basket. Butcher block makes an attractive counter.*

Attractive, practical for adults, children

In its new form, this remodeled 1946 bathroom fills the needs of parents, child, and guests. The shower base is a receptor tub, deep enough to bathe a child in. Storage includes locked drawers, portable baskets, and a pull-out cabinet.

An imported blue and white-patterned tile used for the floor and for detailing accents the cool blue and white color scheme. Natural light enters the bathroom through a square skylight that's fitted with two frosted bulbs for night illumination.

Architect: Michael D. Moyer.

BATHROOMS BEFORE ...AND AFTER

Before: *Inconvenient bathroom had dinky window, improvised storage.*

Adding skylight opens bath to the sky

A 4 by 6-foot skylight brightens and opens up a remodeled bathroom. The skylight exterior can be hosed down from the roof; the inside is cleaned by hand.

This bath is in an 1897 house that had already been remodeled once when the "before" photograph was taken. Fixtures projected into the room, the light level was low, and storage space was inadequate.

The new cabinets are made of overlaid plywood that was oiled, sealed with polyurethane, and trimmed with walnut. Cabinets house a sink, roll-out hamper, cupboards, and 10 drawers.

Architect: Bruce Wendell Beebe.

Now: *Window is covered up and ceiling opened with large skylight. On the left are a standard tub and shower stall.*

Paper, paint create new sophistication

With a minimum of structural change, the bathroom acquired an entirely fresh, new look. First, a projecting wall was removed. Then modern fixtures replaced the old ones, a round skylight was added, the walls were papered in a striking black and white geometric pattern, and a plush red carpet was installed.

Because the owner is tall, the new countertop measures 40 inches high (usual height is 36 inches) and the shower/tub enclosure is oversize.

Inside the bathroom, white built-in cabinets and drawers provide plenty of storage; there's even a hamper built into one wall. Row lights on both sides of the wood-framed mirror supplement the skylight, which includes rheostatted electric lights.

Architect: George Cody. Interior Designer: Stewart Morton.

Before: *Awkward partition was in the way in old-fashioned bathroom.* **View past** *floor-to-ceiling drawers into bath shows new basin area. The mirror on 6-inch projection gives person shaving a close view.*

Display places for plants add life, color

After choosing honey-colored oak for its light and airy effect, the owners of this bathroom decided on tile in a light shade to enhance and harmonize with the wood rather than a dark or bold-patterned tile that would overwhelm it. One continuous wall is finished with tongue-and-groove oak flooring treated with sealer and polyurethane. White cabinetry and fixtures also complement the wood; growing plants provide texture and focal points.

Plants live under slightly different growing conditions in the lavatory area and in the shower room. The planter behind the basin has the advantages of direct sunlight and watering convenience. The tub/shower area tends to have a variable high humidity level, warmer air temperature, and reflected light. The owners rotate pots of flowering plants and experiment with exotics difficult to grow elsewhere in the house.

Architect: Michael D. Moyer.

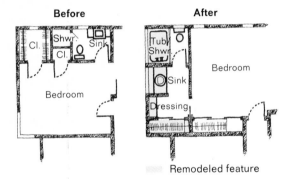

Plans: *More usable than before, master bath and bedroom were remodeled without exterior construction. Moving the plumbing and rearranging walls added elbow room; spaces for plants were incorporated into the design. A total of four rooms (bedroom, dressing room, lavatory area, and tub/toilet compartment) now work smoothly together as a unit.*

Sunken tub/shower *saves space, works well for both showers and baths. It's slightly larger than usual, measuring 3 by 6 feet. The top shelf was designed specifically for plants; the lower shelf—for storing odds and ends—slopes slightly for drainage. Shelves against the window hold more potted plants.*

Suspended mirror *"floats" between basin and built-in, metal-lined planter that has drainage holes to outside.*

Accessories *include a streamlined magazine holder built into the new wall.*

BATHROOMS BEFORE...AND AFTER

1868 tub in a linear bathroom

A shallow lot line directed the design here. The solution to the narrow site was to string out compartments in a linear fashion, creating separate spaces that can be used with privacy.

Duckboard floor sections in both tub and sauna compartments have drains beneath to carry off water. The bay beside the tub allows room for a convenient ledge; the leaded glass window is set at an angle to provide privacy and bring light down to the tub.

Architect: Richard Ehrenberger.

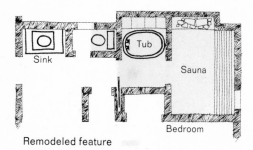

Remodeled feature

Plans: *Toilet compartment, part of the original house, was rotated 90°. Then new compartments for the tub and for the sauna were added on.*

Gleeful little girl *plays with movable shower head (also useful for shampooing and for rinsing the tub). The 1868 tub, designed to conserve space in a maid's room, is deep but only 3½ feet long.*

Now bathroom fills its owners' needs

Remodeled for two working adults, this bathroom is now extremely functional, as well as attractive. It's divided into three activity zones: a corner of washbasins and cabinets; a compartment for the toilet; and a glass-walled enclosure containing a double shower.

The sink area was formerly a closet for the master bedroom; adding this space to the bathroom doubled its size. As part of extensive remodeling, the entire house was replumbed. Separate plumbing lines provide variable temperature and water pressure for each shower head.

The cabinets were designed by Greg Smith, The Just Plain Smith Company.

Before: *Walled off from the house's side yard, bathroom appears small and stuffy.*

Spacious shower enclosure *that replaced a tub looks out to garden through new window wall.*

Two higher-than-usual *antique basins inset in marble countertop sections double efficiency, save time. Collection of mirrors and pictures personalizes the wall above the basins. Gold fixtures and oak cabinets add color and texture.*

Great old tub *with feet was refinished, painted. The enlarged window above it changed the character of the bathroom by giving a new impression of space and movement. From the tub, there's a delightful view to a hillside garden. The slope of the hill and the trees provide privacy.*

New windows *have small panes to match the ones elsewhere in the house; the owner had them made to his specifications and installed them himself. The basin inset in the marble countertop is new.*

Doing their own work and recycling cut costs

A year of searching led to the discovery of this antique French cabinet; the owners planned their bathroom remodeling project around it. They had decided that standard cabinets were dull but that building their own was too expensive. Since the existing bathroom was too small for the cabinet, they pushed a wall out 18 inches to create a cabinet alcove.

After consulting an architect, the owners gutted, rewired, replumbed, and rebuilt the room themselves. It took them about a month of weekends and after-work hours to rip out and do the basics; then it required two months to put the new room together.

Walls, floor, and shower enclosure are built of redwood tongue-and-groove boards (a square-jointed milling so the grooves between the boards meet instead of making a "V"). Six coats of polyurethane sealer and five coats of satin polyurethane protect the wood surfaces.

Architect: James Bell.

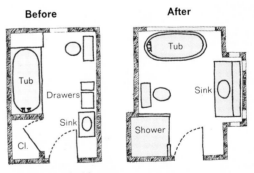

Remodeled feature

Plans: *Built 50 years ago, bathroom in summer home that became a permanent residence had been remodeled in the early 1950s. To relieve the '50s look, fixtures were moved around and important new windows added. Part of an adjoining closet was incorporated into a new shower stall.*

STAINED GLASS TINTS MANY BATHS WITH GLOWING COLOR

Outside the recycled stained-glass window, a light stays on to focus attention on the decorative glass and to illuminate the bathroom at night. Recycled white porcelain handles and hooks add a nostalgic touch to the cedar-lined bathroom. For showers, a curtain fitted with two wood rings stretches between the two hooks on the walls. The owner/designer built the tub (see page 7). Designer: Rick Morrall.

Dark wood interior of small bathroom makes a dramatic setting for a tilt-open stained-glass window. The window's subtle greens, blues, and yellows soften and then shimmer as the light outside changes. A redwood burl counter holds the sink. Architect: William Kirsch.

Vertical mirrors at each end of the tub reflect stained-glass casement windows. The colors used in the stained glass provide a starting point for colors and styles of accessories. Ledge around three sides of the tub is wide enough for plants, ornaments, soap, and bath oil. (Also see page 52.) Architect: Herbert D. Kosovitz; windows designed by David Adams.

40

Rough Douglas fir paneling, *thick and glossy wood counter, glass, ceramics, stone, and flourishing green plants make an oasis of this bath under a skylight. Baskets under the counter hold laundry, miscellaneous items. Shaving mirror pulls out on an accordian-type extension. Skylight extends into the adjoining shower. (See basin closeup on page 43.)*

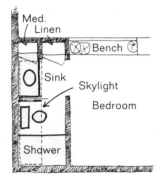

Med.
Linen

Bench

Sink

Skylight

Bedroom

Shower

Plan: *Lavatory section opens to the bedroom; a pocket door separates the toilet and shower compartment. Architect: Herbert D. Kosovitz.*

Under the new wood facade *are the original fixtures, unchanged except that the plumbing for the sink was moved over slightly. The redwood was salvaged from feed troughs; knots and holes were patched with pieces of tin. The north window and reflective ceiling covered with heavy-gauge aluminum foil supplement room's light level. In a plumbing sculpture of narrow copper pipes, faucets are arranged one above the other. The basin, a soy tub made of water-resistant teak, has a protective coat of polyester resin on the bottom. Designer: Al Garvey; tile designed by Lisa Glaser.*

Stained glass brightens *self-contained bathing room, 5 feet square, that connects to "dry" bathroom through sliding door. Smooth-cut, exterior tongue-and-groove cedar covers walls; 6-inch quarry tiles line floor and border base of walls. Floor and walls are treated with waterproofing agents; a plastic film flashing catches any leaks. Three-inch tile ledge extending from rim of tub ensures correct drainage. Architect: Daniel M. Streissguth; window designed by Jean Frantz.*

BASINS AND MIRRORS

Off by itself, *pedestal basin acquires new, graceful quality. Exposed plumbing adds to its sculptural appearance. Mirror, accessories are in same old-fashioned mood. Architect: William Kirsch.*

Stainless steel *sinks were manufactured as bar sinks, and the clean-lined control levers were intended for hospital use. Impressive row of medicine cabinets with backs painted shiny blue is more fun than one long mirror. Overhead row of standard greenhouse glass sections lets in much light; vents open for fresh air. Matchstick bamboo curtains pull across glass if light becomes too intense. Architect: Peter Behn.*

Blue and white chinoiserie
wallpaper matches the porcelain basin; fittings have the look of pewter. Restricting the number of colors used in this bathroom to two creates a sophisticated effect. Architect: Henry Blackard.

Hammered copper basin, *the owner/architect's second attempt at copper work, was shaped by heating sheet copper with an acetylene torch to make it malleable, hammering it, and then crimping the edges. The basin fits in a counter of fir; fittings were sanded with emery paper to give brass finish. (Also see page 47.)*

Hand-thrown *pottery basin suits the design and materials used around it (see page 41). Rounded wooden towel bar extends along front of counter. Basin was designed by Eric Norstad.*

Black trim *accents hexagonal mirror, edge of skylight, cabinet, and a sliding door that's hung on tracks, barn-door style.*

Mirrored wall *extends reflections above double basins, makes bathroom seem larger. Tall, built-in planter, surfaced in pale wood, matches the vanity. Cheery yellow chrysanthemums add color.*

Beautifully detailed *wood-working enriches the basin area. A ceiling-to-floor panel of orange, amber, and ruby stained glass reflects in the mirror. A kitchen sink, big enough to make hair washing easy, was used here instead of a smaller bathroom fixture. A drawer pulls out over the small ledge to the left. Three shelves hinge down to set bottles and brushes on. (Also see page 46.)*

COMBINE YOUR BATHROOM WITH A BEDROOM OR WITH THE OUT-OF-DOORS

Pelicans, the sun, the moon, and the tree of life appear among the mosaic tile motifs on this bathing tub. When the new foundation of the house was poured, a sunken concrete tub was incorporated into the design. The mosaics were set in 12-inch-wide sections and then pressed into a bed of mortar. Behind the louvered panels are a water heater and a swimming pool circulation pump. An interior garden grows in the light well behind the tub. Designed by sculptor Martin Metal.

Tucked between two walls of the house, atrium garden opens to the sky. Curved transparent shower door, curved tub reinforce natural feeling. Architects: Colwell and Ray; Interior Designer: Charles A. Lewis.

In the center of a one-room house, an imposing structure enshrines this tub: tall, wooden columns from an old factory reach to a white vault that opens to a large, flat skylight high in the main roof. Three broad steps/levels descend to the deepest part of the tiled tub.
Architect: Charles Moore.

Built around two trees with wood salvaged from an old barn, this outdoor bathing shelter has a series of skylights in its multibeamed roof. The upper level offers a steaming hot tub with a built-in hydro massage unit and two rock-bordered pools: one pool supplies a quick, cooling dip after a soak in the tub; the other provides a home for fish. Down a few stone steps, a tree screens an outdoor shower; through a heavy wooden door is a large sauna (see back cover). Woodworking by Frank Bitz; stonework by Allan Elder.

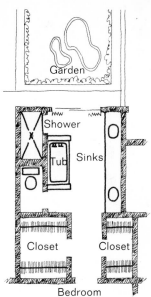

Plan: *Here are compartments with a difference—the wall that forms the main partition performs an additional important decorative function (see photo at left). Architect: William A. Churchill.*

Floor-to-ceiling tile *makes an effective backdrop for the sunken standard tub in this bathing room with a garden view. Louvers of dark wood pull across glass doors.*

Walled-in *but open to the sky, a corner patio links the bedroom and bathroom. The bathroom and patio were added and the bedroom enlarged during a house remodeling. The patio supplies additional private space off the bedroom. In the bathroom the basin fits in a refinished and repaired cabinet; there's a combination tub/shower at the end of the bathroom opposite the door to the patio. Architect: Peter Choate.*

THESE BATHTUBS ARE SPECIAL

Contoured tub bends *around base of 6-foot-high retaining wall. A shower head high on one wall and a step leading down into the tub add convenience. The tub was constructed of ferro-cement and surfaced with smooth stones set in mortar. Concrete underlies the wood walls where they intersect the retaining wall. Large windows bring in natural light; a ceiling of redwood blocks adds to the impression of a natural grotto. Basin, bidet, and toilet are in another compartment (see page 43). Designed by John Morrall and David F. Griffith.*

Bubble window rim *projects about 8 inches, just enough space for a 6-year-old to stand up on. Ideas for this bath developed in Japan: the tub, big enough for two, has a vista into the trees. In keeping with the circle of the bubble window, the cedar wall curves. The cedar, sealed to prevent moisture damage, is nailed to 1/4-inch plywood sheets curved at the corners. Underneath, a metal pan, hot-asphalt-mopped roofing felt, and chicken wire were applied to a shaped frame. Mortar covered the wire and formed the base for tiny mosaic tiles. Colored grout finished the tub's surface. Architects: Burger and Coplans.*

Handbuilt wooden tub *replaced tub and shower in windowless room. The tub was built through the combined efforts of the owner, his two sons, and the designer over a 3-month period. First, the wood foundation was reinforced. Then fiberglass resin coated the plywood tub floor; transparent silicone glue filled spaces between laminated redwood 2 by 4s. Five or 6 coats of spar varnish were applied to coat the tub sides. The rebuilt room walls include large windows; planters were incorporated into the flowing design of the tub. The designer was sculptor Chuck Jaeger.*

Holding twice *as much water as a standard tub, a square tub in an alcove gives the effect of a sunken tub but is built on an upper story. Underneath the tub, a heater helps keep bath water warm while heating the room. Soft, rheostatted overhead lighting and north and west-facing windows illuminate the tub enclosure. (Also see front cover.)*
Architect: Robert Herman.

Gleaming copper tub *measures 5 feet across and 22 inches deep. It's for soaking after using the outdoor shower visible through the glass doors. Under the copper (which was cut and soldered at a sheet metal shop) are layers of sheet plastic, rigid insulation, and tar. The sunken tub fits in a semiprivate space between the master bedroom and the rest of the helix-shaped house. Off to one side, another room contains a clothes closet, toilet, and basin (see page 43).*
Architect: J. Alexander Riley.

Sunny yellow, *easy-to-clean chemical vat forms liner for this outdoor hot tub. Lid in two sections covers tub to keep warmth in, leaves and small children out. Swimming pool heater, pump, and filter freshen hot water.*
Designer: John Fredrick Krumme.

SHOWERS AND SAUNAS

Nautical bathroom with sauna, inside a side door close to a boat dock, makes a great place to clean up and unwind after a cruise. Outer compartment contains a washbasin; through the clear door is a combination shower and sauna room. Quarry tile lines the shower enclosure; the other walls and the floor are wood. Architect: Fred Briggs; Interior Designer: Suzanne Faulkner.

Low wall divides sections of large, easy-to-clean, tiled compartment. Showering and bathing take place in the inner section; a drain in the outer section carries away splashes. The track for the sliding compartment door, far enough away from splashing area, stays dry and clean. The low wall/tub side makes a comfortable seat measuring 19 inches high and 10½ inches wide on a 6-inch concrete base. A ledge for shaving gear and plants tops one 6-foot wall; at this height the ledge stays dry. Designer: Sal Iniquez.

High, narrow window lights sauna room built of light-colored fir. A wood railing shields the wood-burning heater. The benches are staggered to allow three people to stretch out.

Plan: Small building contains sauna, shower, and rest area. A doorway divides the sauna from the rest/shower compartment. Designed by carpenter Forrest Shute.

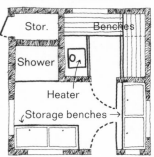

Your bathroom color scheme
...almost anything goes

When you enter a bathroom or when you glance at a photograph of one, color is the first thing you perceive—it speaks louder than form. Color has immediate aesthetic, psychological, and even physiological effects.

Colors stretch the connotations of a room. Color says something to people, based chiefly on their recollections of earlier experiences and on cultural stereotypes. When you look at the bathroom on page 35, you might be reminded of a Mediterranean beach, with clear, blue water washing over clean, white sand. You may conclude that the bathroom on the left of page 40 belongs to a man because dark wood is often associated with masculinity; a pink bathroom would probably seem feminine.

Color can substantially alter a bathroom's character. The way you use color can create patterns and shapes independent of the basic structure of the room, change its apparent size and shape, join places that are separate, or divide a single surface. Part of the reason the bathroom on page 33 looks much larger than it appeared in the "before" picture is the sweep of harmonizing colors on the counter, cabinet, floor, and wall, and the band of colored trim encircling the wall.

Rules for using color are endless and often conflicting. The only really valid rule is to use the colors and combinations of colors that you respond to positively. The key to color scheme success is to find the colors that complement both your emotions and your architectural space.

You can purchase a color wheel—a very useful tool in working with color—at an art supply store or an art school. Colors that appear opposite each other on the wheel are *complementary*. In a complementary color scheme, usually only one color is used at full intensity. The bathroom at the bottom of page 40 illustrates the complementary colors violet and yellow—in quantities small enough that both can be used at full intensity. *Analogous* colors, which are located next to each other on the color wheel, are often used together. The yellows, ambers, oranges, and reds seen in the bathroom at the top right of page 43 compose an analogous color scheme. Three colors equidistant from each other on a color wheel are called a *triad*. The primary colors of red, blue, and yellow make up the most familiar triad (see the bathroom on page 48, top right). A *monochromatic* color scheme uses one color in several different tones, tints, or shades. For an example of an effective monochromatic color scheme, see the use of neutrals in the bathroom on the left of page 45.

To avoid mistakes in using color, view all the shades you're considering under the same type of light you'll have in your bathroom and with all coordinating materials (including wood, metals, and porcelain). We have no true color memory, so unless you have all your samples together to make comparisons, you can't make an accurate judgment. Since color is produced by light waves striking pigmented surfaces, colors change with the time of day and with the degree and type of artificial lighting.

The manufacturers recommend that you not try to match fixture colors exactly. Because floors and counter-tops aren't changed very often, they should be selected carefully to harmonize with the color of the fixtures. The same is true of walls if they're to be surfaced with permanent materials such as ceramic tile or plastic laminate. Painted walls will probably be redecorated every 4 or 5 years, so you can select colors more freely for these surfaces. You'll want to vary towels and accessories in new colors and patterns—don't limit the choices by using too much pattern or too many colors in the more permanent elements of the room.

Flowing pattern of green leaves and fronds, handpainted on cream-colored tile, surrounds tub. Architect: Edward Carson Beall; tile designed by Barbara Vantrease Beall.

The finishing touches

- **Mirrors**
- **Storage**
- **Towel racks, towels**
- **Fittings**
- **Tub/shower curtains and doors**

Mirrors, cabinets, faucets and handles, shower curtains, and towels give a bathroom personality. They're comparatively easy to change to suit an owner's taste. And they're important to the overall appearance and style of a bathroom.

Select these accessories on the basis of the effect you want to achieve in your bathroom, considering also how water will affect them and whether they can be cleaned easily.

Look through bath departments of large stores, bathroom specialty shops, hardware stores, and manufacturers' catalogues to gather ideas for accessories that will make your bathroom more attractive, efficient, and individual.

Mirrors offer high style

Both decorative and utilitarian, mirrors can make a bathroom seem much brighter and more spacious. They can serve as substitute windows in a small, windowless bathroom, while performing their main function as an aid to good grooming.

Bathroom mirrors should be backed with high-quality electroplated copper to prevent steam from affecting the silvering. Clean them often because soap caught between the frame and the glass will, over a period of time, corrode the mirror.

Full-length mirrors can be mounted on a wall or a door. A mirror mounted on a door should be securely fastened so that closing the door doesn't cause it to shift or fall. Full-length mirrors that swing out from a wall can conceal storage space.

Three-way mirrors let the user see his profile and the back of his head. Mirrors placed on opposite walls help in seeing all sides. Also available are mirrors that swing into position for use and then move out of the way. Mirrors can also be slanted for easier viewing.

Mirrored medicine cabinet doors have long been standard. When you remove an old medicine cabinet, it's quite easy to install a newer, more decorative, mirrored cabinet in the opening or to install a cabinet with a mirror on the inside of the door. Mirrors can also serve as sliding panel doors for cabinets.

If a separate mirror is hung over the lavatory, the top of the mirror should be at least 72 inches from the floor for easy viewing by tall people. An 8-inch space is usually left between the top of the counter and the bottom of the mirror as a backsplash. Most integral bowl lavatories made of synthetic marble come with a 4-inch splash. With these, the mirror can be brought down to the top of the splash and sealed with silicone. In double basin installations, an oversize mirror provides easy viewing for more than one person at a time. Lavatories built into an island structure to serve two people might have two mirrors mounted back-to-back. If the lavatory is beneath a window, a mirror can be hinged to the adjacent wall so that it swings into place above the basin and then swings back to allow a view.

Mirrors of glass or reflective acrylic can be fastened with mirror clips or J-molding or by drilling through the glass or acrylic and then using screws and washers to hold the mirror in place.

Storage: cabinets and cupboards

Storage space—for towels, soap, toiletries, medicines, hair dryers, electric shavers—is necessary in any bathroom. In large bathrooms, of course, there are more possibilities for including storage space. But even in the tiniest bathroom, efficient storage is possible.

If you're planning a new bathroom, try this system for supplying storage: 1) List the items for which storage space is required, even if they're stored for only a brief time. 2) Separate the items into categories—those that can be kept within view, small items, large ones requiring capacious storage, things that need to be locked up. 3) Estimate the amount of space needed to hold the items in each category. 4) Draw the required storage space into the bathroom plan.

Mirror set at angle *for easy viewing fits in narrow space below window. Architects: Phillips and Dumlao.*

Long, narrow mirror *above oversize tub makes bathroom appear even larger and reflects dark pink wall color. Architect: Herbert D. Kosovitz.*

Built-in storage *combines hinge-up mirror and ample laundry hamper.*

Combination *vanity/washing center can serve two people. Four mirror sections —one double-sided—give maximum view. Architects: Rhinehart & Durr.*

Overhead mirror *reflects light back into shaving area, eliminating some shadows. Mirror also seems to open room to second floor. Designer: Priscilla Fontana.*

Medicine cabinets

The most familiar type of medicine cabinet is mounted on, or recessed into, the wall above the lavatory and usually has a hinged, mirrored door. More elaborate medicine cabinets have different styles of doors, built-in lighting fixtures, and outlets for electric shavers, hair dryers, or other bathroom appliances. Some have wing mirrors for three-way vision. Cabinets are available in a variety of sizes; custom-built medicine cabinets, of course, can be made any size. A locked medicine cabinet or a locking compartment within the cabinet is a wise precaution for families with children.

Medicine cabinets don't have to be located over the lavatory. When large mirrors are used over the wash basin, the medicine cabinet is often on a wall to the side. Or a pair of cabinets may be used, each on a different wall. If a lavatory cabinet has sufficient drawer and cabinet space built in under the counter, a portion of this unit may be used as a medicine cabinet, making an above-counter cabinet unnecessary. Twin and triple medicine cabinets can relieve overcrowded conditions. In smaller bathrooms, corner cabinets save space.

Inside a medicine cabinet, shelves 4 to 6 inches apart will hold most tubes, jars, and bottles; one shelf should allow at least 9 inches for taller bottles.

A recessed medicine cabinet of almost any size can be built into a new bathroom. In an existing bathroom, installing a larger or an additional recessed cabinet can be more difficult because of in-place studs, pipes, and electric wiring—all expensive to move.

Surface-mounted cabinets are easier to install during remodeling, but they're more obtrusive and take up more of the space that's so valuable in a small bathroom. If the front of a surface-mounted cabinet is mirrored, the mirror is more difficult to light properly than one that's flush with the wall. Surface-mounted cabinets, though, are less likely to transmit sound through walls than recessed ones.

Lavatory cabinets

Cabinets with an inset sink should be a foot or more wider than the basin itself to be useful for storage. Otherwise the plumbing takes up too great a proportion of space. In small cabinets (less than 44 inches wide) avoid centering the basin; an off-center basin frees more storage space.

The simplest type of lavatory cabinet is a box with a slot cut in the back to allow for the drainpipe. Stock vanities are available with various arrangements of cabinets, shelves, and drawers; they come in various widths but are usually restricted to a few standard heights and depths. Modular cabinet sections can be joined under a single countertop, with filler pieces used where necessary to obtain a specific length. You could

Decorative towel ring *on door of cabinet also serves as handle to open medicine cabinet that's recessed in wall above tiled splashback. Architect: William A. Churchill.*

Lipped shelves *inside flush door double cabinet's capacity. Varying distances between shelves accommodate variety of medicines, sundries. Architect: Herbert D. Kosovitz.*

Style of antique cabinet *built into corner of bathroom complements pottery basin with matte-finish fittings. Architect: Herbert D. Kosovitz.*

Tall cabinet *with stacked drawers fits in corner of bathroom's dressing area. Interior Designer: Carol Gordon.*

Cut-out center drawer *allows space for new sink; plastic laminate top cleans easily. Interior Designer: Carol Weiss.*

also leave a knee space to allow you to sit at the counter. Styles of prebuilt models are almost exclusively traditional; imitation wood and white finishes predominate. If you prefer a cabinet in a different style or need a different storage arrangement or different dimensions, you'll probably have to have one built by a cabinetmaker.

Other storage possibilities

In a large bathroom, an entire wall could be attractively designed to contain storage space. This wall could be a combination of cabinets, closets, drawers, and shelves to suit your specific needs. Dividers that create compartments in a large bathroom or screen off fixtures often can include cabinets and shelves.

Where space is at a premium, built-ins are the best storage providers. If you can't include built-ins, try to utilize every square foot of wall space. You might add pole units hung with open shelves and small cabinets.

Suspended 1½ feet above floor, simple plywood lavatory cabinet takes up minimum space, makes small bathroom appear more spacious. Architect: John Schmid.

Adjustable poles *hung with shelves and cabinets can conserve space, provide storage in small bath.*

Among other possibilities are wall-hung shelves and hanging shelves suspended from the ceiling, singly or in tiers. Perhaps you can fit more storage between the medicine cabinet and the ceiling, over the toilet tank, and above the tub.

For things you use every day, open storage is a good alternative. Try shelves, rods, and hooks for those things you don't mind leaving out.

For storing large items, a cabinet 12 inches deep and at least 12 inches wide works well. Drawers of varying depths are convenient. Shelves and cabinets need be only 8 to 10 inches deep to store bath towels and other supplies. If this size shelf or cabinet is set in between the studs, it will project into the room only 4 to 6 inches.

A bathroom clothes hamper is an added convenience. This could be a wide basket on wheels or simply a large basket that's stored inside a bathroom cabinet or closet. Built-in hampers with removable liners are also convenient.

Clothes hamper *under sinks drops open on heavy chain attached to lavatory island. Pegboard bottom ventilates hamper. Architect: Leonard Veitzer.*

Two rows *of slide-out rods hold towels dried by warmth from heater duct running through vertical cabinet. Architect: J. Lloyd Conrich.*

Towel racks and towels

Towels in exciting, bright new colors and patterns add an extra dimension to bathroom decorating. They're beautiful as well as functional: a stack of colorful towels can be a decorative asset. Additional hues and patterns appear every year, often with matching accessories.

Cotton terry cloth and cotton and synthetic blends effectively absorb water. Towel textures vary from rough, nubbly, looped surfaces to velvety-soft plush finishes. But sizes can vary too—before buying a set of towels, be sure to unfold them, for not all "bath towels" have the same dimensions.

You could store towels on an open shelf or use a wicker basket as a portable linen closet—air circulating around the towels will keep them fresh.

Ideally, you should provide one 36-inch towel bar for each person using the bathroom. This gives ample space for a folded bath towel, hand towel, and wash cloth. Bars just for face towels should be at least 18 inches long; bars for bath towels, at least 24 inches. A convenient towel bar height for adults is 36 to 42 inches above floor level.

If you don't have much room to hang towels, try putting towel bars in out-of-the-ordinary locations. You could place towel bars one above the other on a wall, setting the lower one on a line with the lavatory and the other at least 26 inches higher (so you can dry a large bath towel on the upper bar). Another way to hang two or more sets of towels on limited wall space is to install two towel ladders side by side or put towel bars on the sides of cabinets or on cabinet doors. Swinging bars and pull-out extension bars save space too.

Towel rings, hooks, and converted coat racks take up less space than bars and are handy for supplemental towel and washcloth storage, but towels dry faster when they're spread out on bars. Be sure to put any hooks above or below eye level.

For a touch of luxury, consider heated towel racks that dry the towels quickly and keep them warm.

Place towels where they'll be easy to reach when you need them, but avoid installing a towel bar next to a shower where towels will be soaked by the spray.

Screwing or nailing a towel bar, ring, or hook to the wall is more permanent than using adhesives. Even if your bathroom walls are tiled, holes can be drilled for screws.

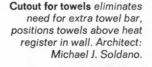

Towels hung *across louvered door dry surprisingly fast, stay fresh.*

Cutout for towels *eliminates need for extra towel bar, positions towels above heat register in wall. Architect: Michael J. Soldano.*

One holder *for adults, lower one for children attach to same wall. Horizontal pieces are 2 by 2s held out from wall by 4½-inch-long 2 by 3s. Six-inch-long lag bolts hold them together and to wall.*

Water-resistant *liquid plastic protects double towel bars. Shallow holes drilled in mounts made from 2 by 12 scrap seat 1½-inch dowels. Screws with finishing washers hold each mount to wall.*

Fittings for fixtures

Fittings—faucets and handles—add the finishing touch to the plumbing fixtures installed in your new or remodeled bathroom, and they should be selected with care. Bathtubs and basins are often sold without fittings. This way, you can select the fitting style that will best complete your decorating plan, and you also have full control over the expense.

Fittings for plumbing fixtures come in budget, quality, and deluxe types. Some lavatory fittings are very inexpensive; others are quite costly. In general, it's poor economy to buy cheap fittings because they are likely to wear out quickly. It's also advisable to avoid off-brands or "bargain" fittings because of the difficulty in securing replacement parts later.

The price of fittings depends on the quality of brass used in their manufacture and the internal operating mechanism. Most fittings now available feature all-brass construction in basic parts.

Fittings are available finished in chrome, acrylic, plastic, gold, or porcelain. Monogrammed and colored handles are luxurious touches.

If you're replacing fittings, you must turn off the water that passes through them by turning the supply line cut-off valve—these valves should be installed with each plumbing fixture. The valves often are in the wall or in a closet or room adjoining the bathroom.

Double-handle controls *come in many styles and in a variety of materials.*

Sink fittings

Fittings for lavatories are of two basic types—single-handle and double-handle controls. Decide which type of control you prefer and then make sure the mechanism will fit on the sink you've chosen. The number of holes in the sink and the distances between them determine which fittings can be used with that particular sink. If you plan to attach fittings to a wall or a counter, design the hole arrangement to suit the fittings.

Some fittings have a built-in drain stop mechanism; others require a separate plug. Sink fittings are available with spray attachments, dispensers for soap or lotion, and spouts that swing to the side. Dial controls are available; aerator attachments ensure an even water flow.

Some manufacturers claim their lavatory fittings will operate for the life of a house without dripping.

If you're replacing sink fittings, a single-handle

faucet will usually fit onto the present plumbing for single or double faucets. Before buying a new unit, measure the center-to-center distance between the holes in the sink where the faucet fits. This will tell you the center-to-center distance between the supply pipes —it will be either 4, 6, or 8 inches. Ask for a new faucet assembly with the same centers.

Single-lever *(or knob) control adjusts both water temperature and force.*

Tub and shower fittings

Fittings for a bathtub include single or double-handle controls and a spout—sometimes with a built-in drain stop. A shower has a shower head and a control. Combination tub/showers have a tub spout, a shower head, a double or single-handle control, and a transfer valve that diverts water to the shower head.

Constant-temperature controls (mixing valves) prevent sudden bursts of hot or cold water. With this type of control, you dial the temperature you want and the unit maintains this temperature. Some units even shut off automatically if the hot or cold-water supply fails or if the water drops below a certain temperature; then they restore the flow of water when the pressure returns.

A specialized type of shower assembly has shower heads at two different heights. The heads can be used singly or together.

Or you could purchase separate shower heads and set them at any height or angle you'd like. With shower

Fitting set *for tub/shower includes shower head, control, spout and diverter.*

heads on opposite walls, you can stand between them for a unique kind of shower. Using separate plumbing, you could adjust each one for a different temperature, force, and direction of spray.

Some shower heads are self-cleaning—water rushes through the interior of the head to prevent clogging. Most shower heads are also equipped with a small knob that adjusts the water flow. Other shower heads give a wider range of speed and direction of water. Mixers attach to the shower head to dispense soap, gel, shampoo, or oil with the water.

If you're replacing tub and shower faucets, the replacements must fit the faucet body behind the wall. If the faucet assembly is an old one, you might have trouble finding new handles to fit onto the body. In that case you're in for more complicated work—you'll have to get behind the wall and replace the faucet body as well. To assure correct size, take the old faucet body with you when you buy the new one.

Tub and shower curtains, doors

While serving the practical purpose of keeping water from splashing on the floor, shower curtains can also add a note of color and pattern, and shower doors can present a graceful sweep of glass or plastic.

Glass and plastic enclosures, though less decorative than brightly hued shower curtains, are more watertight and offer better support if a bather should slip.

Shower curtains

Temporary shower curtains can be hung on spring-tension rods that are easy to put up and take down. This is an especially good arrangement if you take a bath more often than you shower.

The curtain itself is an inexpensive item that can be replaced often to create a new look. You can use sheets or almost any fabric, hung with a separate piece of vinyl that protects the fabric from water. Or the fabric itself can be waterproofed—do this with a spray product manufactured for the purpose, or have it done by a

drycleaner. Remember, you'll be looking at both sides of the curtain; it should be attractive from all angles.

Shower doors

Metal-framed glass or plastic panels are popular as tub/shower doors. They're available in many patterns to fit showers and tubs of varying dimensions—you can even find special doors for corner showers.

Most houses built within the last 10 years have safety glass in the shower doors, installed because of code requirements. However, older homes are likely to contain shower doors glazed with ¼-inch translucent glass, which will resist a moderate blow but will splinter if struck by a falling body.

Hazardous glass can be replaced either in the frame with approved safety glass or acrylic plastic or with a whole new code-approved door.

Tub enclosures are available in three styles: horizontal sliding panels, vertical sliding panels, and accordion-fold plastic closures.

Horizontal sliding panels, glazed with either tempered glass or plastic, have been standard for many years. They're easy to install, repair, and replace. Disadvantages: There's no smooth tub edge, and the fixed panel blocks off half the tub at all times, burdening the soaker in the tub with an imprisoned feeling and restricting elbow room for cleaning the tub or bathing a child, pet, or invalid.

Plastic vertical-sliding panels that raise and lower like double-hung windows offer unobstructed access to the tub. But they're more complicated to install, must be precisely aligned to avoid sticking, and may not be as watertight. The doors are not as widely available as the horizontal style, and replacement parts may not be as easy to find.

Accordion-fold installations offer one decided advantage: the folded panels store at one end, compressed into a compact bundle that takes up a minimum amount of space, easing cleaning and washing operations and eliminating bathtub claustrophobia. Disadvantages: Generally not as watertight as sliding panels, they may

Horizontal sliding

Vertical sliding

Accordion fold

The choice in shower doors

Some shower doors can be installed in only half an hour. Frames come with adjustable flanges to accommodate out-of-plumb walls.

Appliquéd fabric design sewn on a white sheet makes one-of-a-kind shower curtain. Clear plastic liner protects curtain from splashes. Designer: Judy Hanshue Lozano.

Sandwiching curtain rail between two pieces of oiled redwood continues wood motif across front of shower.

Concealed behind tissue holder, compartment stores eight more rolls. Architects: Akiyama, Kekoolani.

Portable rack that holds soap, washcloth—perhaps a magazine, too—adds to convenience in tub. Grab bar on wall aids bather in entering and exiting.

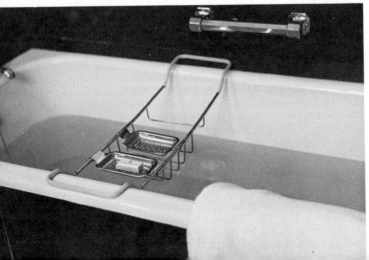

leak and wear around the hinges. Being made of plastic, they're not as rugged or long-lived as glass. Servicing may be difficult, but the folding panels should give several years' service before beginning to wear.

Other accessories

A bathroom without basic accessories would be like a living room without tables and lamps. Accessories add convenience, utility, and an extra spark to the bathroom, and they should be chosen as carefully as the fixtures themselves. Bath accessories come in different price ranges and styles. The basic accessories needed in every bathroom are a holder for toothbrushes and tumbler, a paper holder (recessed in the wall or hung on the wall surface), grab bars, and soap dishes.

Grab bars are practical safety measures for tubs and showers. A straight grab bar in a shower should be about 48 inches above floor level. For a tub that is also used as a shower, there's an angled grab bar shaped like an L. The bottom of the bar should be about 24 inches above floor level for safety while either bathing or showering. For strength, grab bars should be of metal, solidly anchored to wall studs to withstand sudden pulls.

Soap dishes can be recessed in the wall or mounted flush. A soap dish for a bathtub should be at least 24 inches above floor level. In a shower stall, it might be 48 to 54 inches above floor level. In ceramic installations, soap dishes often have built-in grab bars. These should be considered supplemental to metal grab bars.

Additional accessories can be built in to make a bath more comfortable and usable. Such things as magazine racks, scales, hampers, sun lamps, whirlpool units, and drying lines add convenience.

Towels and small accessories are often the most colorful part of bathroom decorating. Since they can be changed more easily and less expensively than any other item in the bathroom, they can provide brilliant colors, accent colors, or a color that might be fashionable this year and out-of-date three or four years from now. Wastepaper baskets and tissue holders, drinking glasses and soap dishes, all are available in exotic colors and designs.

When shopping for accessories, don't limit yourself to the bath shop. Pottery cannisters made for kitchen use can hold bath salts; a dish from an antique store can hold soap. If you want matching accessory sets, though, a bath shop is the place to find them.

Don't forget pictures as bathroom accessories. Proper framing can protect a favorite print from moisture as it adds just the right touch to a bathroom's decor.

Sculpture, a collection of seashells, framed butterflies, posters, a group of small mirrors, unusual containers for soap or guest towels—all add to the charm of a bathroom.

If your bath accessories include radios, television sets, and other electrical accessories, plan their locations carefully to prevent contact with water, and be sure every member of the family is aware of the necessary safety precautions.

Small & half-baths

- **If you have limited space…**
- **Choosing a location**
- **Bathrooms can look larger**
- **Half-baths**

Fitting a convenient, attractive bathroom into a crowded, barely adequate space is an all-too-familiar problem for many homeowners. When the space is limited, the number of possible fixture arrangements and floor plans is also limited. But you can use smaller fixtures or fixtures that fit into corners to help relieve the crowded conditions.

Substituting a half-bath for a full bathroom with a tub or shower can be a workable solution to space problems. Sometimes, even where space isn't a problem, an attractive half-bath is preferable to a full bathroom.

In this chapter are photographs of full bathrooms in which problems of limited space have been solved in different ways, as well as half-baths that are particularly well designed.

Small bathrooms

A small bathroom that's auxiliary to a main bathroom should be designed and decorated to suit its location and principal function. If, for example, this room is adjacent to the garage and is used as a mud room for youngsters and gardeners, it might include a painted concrete floor with a floor drain and an easy-to-clean, non-staining basin and counter. If the main bathroom includes a bathtub, an easy way to save space in a small auxiliary bathroom is to construct a shower only.

Light colors tend to make any small bathroom appear larger and brighter. In a confined bathroom, a little of a strong color can go a long way. Light colors also contribute to the general room illumination.

A white ceiling is often a good choice for a small bathroom. White reflects more light than other colors and visually enlarges a room. If you choose a wood ceiling or one painted in a dark color, plan to provide more lighting to counteract the lower reflection given by a darker ceiling.

Space-stretching features such as a large mirror or a skylight can help overcome the claustrophobic effect of a small bathroom. A sliding pocket door takes up less space than the usual hinged door.

Four possible floor plans for typical small bathrooms are illustrated. Two of the bathrooms contain a tub; the other two have only a shower stall. Two floor plans are suitable for locations with plumbing in one wall; the other two utilize plumbing pipes in two walls.

Well-designed half-baths

Because of the limited space required by a minimal half-bath (it can be as small as 4 by 4 feet and still be practical), it's easier to find room for a new half-bath than for a new full bathroom with a shower or a bathtub. Closets, space under the stairs, or perhaps a corner of a family room are likely candidates for conversion to a half-bath. Plumbing runs to such areas may be a problem, but because a new half-bath usually costs somewhat less than a full bathroom, additional plumbing costs may be offset.

(Continued on page 60)

Wide windows *seem to enlarge bathroom. Extra shower curtain opens to let light in from outside, closes for privacy. Architect: Ray Zambrano.*

Create myriad reflections *and an apparently endless stream of lights by placing mirrors on three sides of vanity. Designer: Bill Nilsen.*

Four small bathroom floor plan ideas

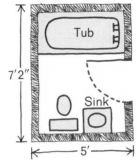

Economical *and compact bathroom plan uses just one wall of plumbing.*

More open arrangement *consumes same square footage, two walls of plumbing.*

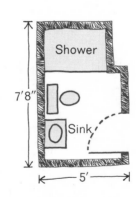

Shower stall *instead of a bathtub takes up less space, even when shower is slightly oversize.*

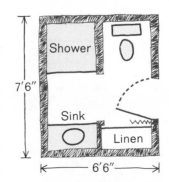

Addition *of a linen closet adds extra utility to this small bathroom with shower.*

(Continued from page 58)

A half-bath handy to the main living areas of a house can serve guests and also give a family additional bathroom facilities. If the half-bath is to be primarily a powder room for adults and their guests, its decor can be more formal and luxurious than that of the family bathroom. On the other hand, if the half-bath is near the kitchen or family room, it may be often used by children and should be planned with easy maintenance in mind.

Because the planning for a new half-bath is practically dictated by the space available, it's quite easy to obtain an estimate of the costs involved.

The half-bath may be a place to try decorating ideas you've always wanted to use but never dared to try. Since no one stays in the room very long, you can be much more dashing than in any other room in the house.

Because moisture isn't as great a problem in a half-bath as in a bathroom containing a tub or shower, you have more freedom in selecting wall and floor materials.

Three basic half-bath arrangements that can be adapted to fit a variety of situations appear at right. Each uses a small space efficiently. The measurements indicate absolute minimums, however; an extra 6 to 12 inches added onto any of the room dimensions will make the half-bath more comfortable and give you more options on fixture arrangement. A bit of extra space could also permit such improvements as double basins, a wider counter around the lavatory, or a partition separating the fixtures.

Three basic half-baths

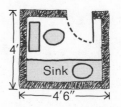

Corner lavatory *saves about 6 inches of wall space in this square bathroom.*

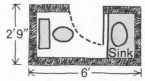

Positioning *the two fixtures on different walls frees space for long counter.*

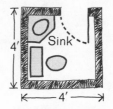

Simple *rectangular bath might fit in a former closet or other narrow space.*

Reflective foil wallpaper *and effective mirror placement make this half-bath seem larger. Behind the extra-wide counter, a built-in planter sheathed in copper holds plants that screen a small window. Architect: Michael D. Moyer.*

Horizontal bands *of harmonizing colors in varying thicknesses add to apparent width of tall, narrow half-bath. Interior Decorator: Orlando Diaz.*

Before: *Worn and corroded sink and tiles (vintage 1942) were difficult to clean. Room appeared small and cramped.*

In process: *Oversize channel-lock pliers eased owner's installation of new sink and vanity.*

After: *Tub and toilet remain; sink and vanity, wall coverings of exterior plywood and water-repelling vinyl, lighting, and foam-backed bath carpet were added in remodeling.*

Lacking space *for a separate stall shower, owner built a wall at open end of tub for the shower plumbing and then bridged across top of tub/shower combination. Architect: James A. Jennings.*

Extra shelf—*a streamlined walnut counter—extends over top of toilet tank; other counter section cantilevers out from wall, holds basin and plumbing.*

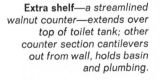

Family & master baths

- **Family bathrooms**
- **Master bathrooms**
- **Compartmentalizing a bathroom**

Each member of a family has specialized requirements in a bathroom. Sometimes six or more people must all share one bathroom—a family bathroom—that meets everyone's needs, including those of young children and the elderly.

If a family is going to add a bathroom, the most popular choice is to place it adjacent to the master bedroom. A master "suite"—consisting of the master bedroom, a dressing room, and a bathroom—is often the result.

Dividing a bathroom into compartments, an efficient way of making one bathroom serve two or more people better, is a popular design solution for both master bedroom-bathroom-dressing room combinations and for whole-family bathrooms.

Whole-family bathrooms

It's commonly recommended that full bathrooms used by families measure at least 5 by 8 feet. This permits use of standardized rough plumbing and the usual fixtures, including a 5-foot bathtub. If a shower is used instead of a tub, the room can be smaller and still be adequate.

A family bathroom is generally located between two bedrooms and across from a third or fourth bedroom. This type of bath can have a door connecting with one of the bedrooms and another door opening off the hallway to serve other bedrooms.

Provisions for children

Most houses don't have special bathrooms for children, but many houses have bathrooms than can be adapted to meet the special needs of children.

Families with young children may choose to increase the size of a family bathroom to 7 by 10 feet or larger to accommodate twin lavatories, a surface for dressing babies, or added storage.

Much baby care takes place in the bathroom. A counter at one end of a lavatory can make bathing an infant easier; diapers, baby lotions and other supplies can be stored in a cabinet under the counter.

Because the bathroom often attracts small children as a temporary play area, medicines and other potentially harmful objects should be kept out of their reach and locked away.

Any bathroom used by children should be planned so that it can be cleaned easily. Carpeting generally isn't practical in a children's bath.

Standard-size fixtures can be made easier for children to use. Special steps will make the lavatory easier to reach, or a sturdy bottom drawer of a cabinet under the basin can be made into a pullout step. Some families find that a drinking fountain is helpful in a bathroom used by children.

A bathroom used primarily by children can be decorated for their enjoyment in a bright and colorful way. Floor and wall designs can be appealing to children, and towels and curtains can be selected to help create a child-pleasing environment. Accessories are easy to change as a child grows older.

(Continued on page 64)

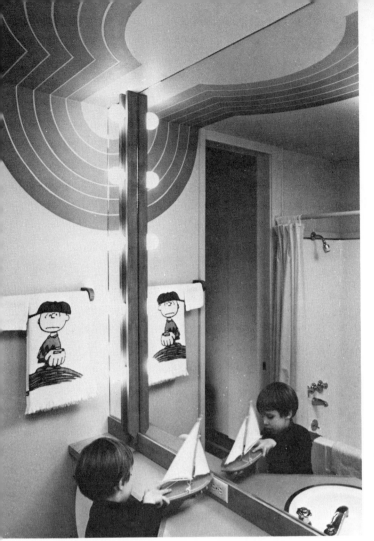

Colorful graphic, *repeated in mirror, livens bathroom occupied by small boy.*

Just the right height *for a 3-year-old, mirror encourages hair combing. Adhesive pads hold square mirror section on wall.*

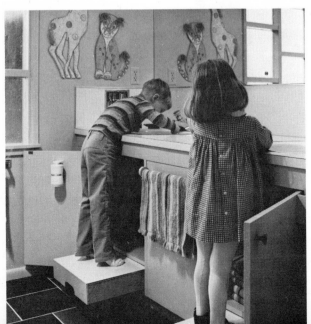

Pull-out steps *(actually plywood drawers used bottom-side up) permit children to reach basins. Between basins, tilt-out laundry bin has dowel handle that's also a child-height towel bar.*

Floor plan variations for family bathrooms

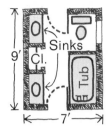

Two basins, *separated by a closet, let two people wash hands at same time.*

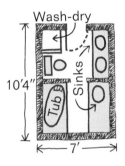

Useful additions *to standard bathroom facilities include a drip-dry compartment and extra counter space for baby care.*

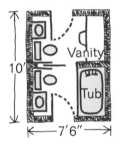

Separate doors *lead into double bath having a convenient dressing table.*

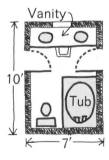

Oversize tub *and twin lavatories fit comfortably into roomy bath. Chair slides underneath counter.*

(Continued from page 62)

Tips that will help you plan a children's bathroom include the following:

- Locks on bathroom doors should be the type that can be opened from the outside in an emergency.
- A night light should be provided.
- A bathroom at ground level can serve as a mud room if there's an outside entrance.
- Children find single-lever faucets easiest to operate.
- Towel racks and toothbrush holders for smaller children should be located where they can be reached easily.
- Electrical appliances should be out of reach or stored away when not in use. Electrically operated toys should be banned from the bathroom.
- A bathroom used by children should be as near to their bedroom as possible.

Provisions for the elderly

The elderly and the infirm often require special consideration in bathroom arrangement. FHA and other housing authorities have very strict requirements for bathrooms used by the handicapped. Bathroom fixtures are available that are designed specifically for use by persons confined to wheelchairs. Hydraulic devices are available for assisting a person into the bathtub, and many shower units and bathtubs are available with built-in seats.

In addition, wall outlets mounted 18 inches from the floor and storage space positioned between knee and shoulder height will reduce the need to stoop and stretch. Grab bars can be located in the shower and tub and next to the toilet. Illumination should be brighter than average, and a permanent night light should be installed.

You might also consider building a doorway wide enough for a wheelchair and using non-slip flooring.

Before: *17-year-old bathroom accommodated only one person, gave limited storage space.*

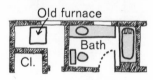

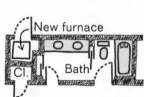

Plans: *Original bathroom was small; furnace room alongside had considerable wasted space. Furnace was relocated, given exterior door.*

After: *Two wash basins were added, along with generous storage below and on one wall. Pocket door connects second compartment containing tub and toilet; each compartment has separate access to hallway.*

Wide step *up to tub serves also as handy bench or shelf.*

Integrating bath, bedroom, and dressing room

The master bedroom becomes a master suite when a bathroom is added. A master bathroom can be either an integral part of the bedroom or separate but adjoining. Placing a tub right in the bedroom is increasingly popular.

A dressing room area, sometimes complete with a basin and extensive cabinets, is often included in this type of bath-bedroom combination. Many master bathrooms have two lavatories to allow use by two people at the same time. Installing a lavatory in the bedroom may be a practical way of gaining an additional fixture when there's not enough room in the bathroom to install another one conveniently.

Tubs and sinks can be separated from the bedroom proper with partial walls, dividers, or screens. Continuation of the bedroom wall and floor coverings into the dressing room and bathroom area will unify the rooms and make them appear larger.

Master bathrooms often incorporate an adjacent garden—and a garden view can do much to make the master suite a relaxing retreat away from the activity of the rest of the house. You may even want to include a sauna or exercise equipment in a master bathroom-bedroom complex.

Most master suites are created during new construction. Still, an existing bathroom can be enlarged, and older homes often have enough space to allow the installation of a lavatory in the bedroom.

Cutaway wall *in dressing room section of bath lets room share space with hall. High windows admit light. Architect: Weldon Jean Skirvin.*

Ideas for master bathrooms

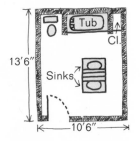

Island *of back-to-back lavatories has mirrors above.*

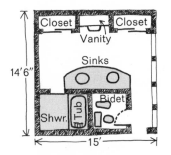

Combination *bath/dressing room contains two closets.*

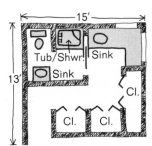

Dressing area *connects bath with master bedroom.*

Compartmentalizing a bath

Compartmentalizing a bathroom—dividing it with solid walls, dividers, sliding screens, or other structures that separate the bathroom fixtures—can make it more usable. Partitioned bathrooms are particularly convenient in homes having one bathroom that must be used by all members of the family, but many master bedroom-bathroom combinations are also sectioned in this way.

One type of compartmentalizing uses partitions within a bathroom having the usual number of fixtures. This might involve simply partitioning the toilet area. On a larger scale, creating a tub and toilet compartment at the rear of the room and an outer lavatory compartment right off the hall would provide convenience and privacy for two or more family members at the same time. This is an especially popular arrangement in a master bedroom suite, where the outer lavatory compartment serves as a dressing room, too. More elaborate arrangements can involve a separate compartment for each fixture.

A different type of compartmentalizing encompasses total area planning. The idea is to give two or three-bath service by adding one or two extra fixtures and a few extra doors. For example, three compartments between two bedrooms could contain a lavatory serving the first bedroom, a shared bathtub and toilet, and another lavatory for the second bedroom.

Compartments in a bathroom also can extend the use of the room to include a washer-dryer area or to provide a special enclosure for hanging hand laundry that's done in the bathroom. Some bathrooms near a back or garage door have a mud room compartment. A small photo darkroom could be located in a compartment adjacent to the bathroom since the water lines for such a room could be connected to the bathroom plumbing system economically.

Special thought must be given to light, heat, and ventilation when the bathroom is divided into compartments. Individual compartments can be separately illuminated, or a luminous ceiling can provide lighting for all the compartments. Suitable venting must be arranged in the shower and toilet compartments. Heating generally isn't much of a problem unless the compartments are quite large, in which case individual heating outlets should be provided. Built-in electric heaters, thermostatically controlled, are good providers of fast heat in small spaces. Generally, portable heaters aren't a good idea since the space within most compartments is too confining for them to be entirely safe.

One key to a successful divided bath is the type and location of doors. Pocket, sliding, or folding doors can be used to conserve wall space.

Often an older home has a large bathroom that lends itself well to partitioning. If an existing bathroom is being remodeled to provide compartments, additional plumbing may be necessary. In many compartmentalized baths, there are two lavatories and two toilets, and it's not always possible to have the plumbing run along a single wall. However, all water lines are located in a compact area, and you can provide three-bath service with possibly four or five fixtures instead of nine.

A designer or architect can help you achieve maximum use with compartmentalizing, and your plumber can also guide you to economical solutions.

Storage divider *separates two lavatories in a combination bath/dressing room. Divider incorporates a cushioned bench and full-length mirror. Architects: Kirk, Wallace, McKinley.*

Towel rack *of 1-inch-square metal tubing rises from floor to ceiling, acts as safety screen for step-down shower. Louvered door, beyond, separates toilet. Architects: Vladimir Ossipoff and Associates.*

An assortment of compartmentalized baths

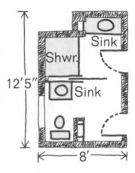

12'5"

8'

Shwr.

Sink

Sink

Close *the pocket door, and one side of this bathroom becomes a half-bath.*

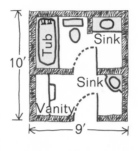

10'

9'

Tub

Sink

Sink

Vanity

Outer area *allows for quick hair combing and hand washing; inner room contains rest of fixtures.*

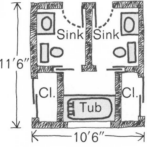

11'6"

10'6"

Sink   Sink

Cl.   Cl.

Tub

Three people *could use this bath at the same time; two closets fit compactly.*

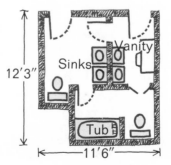

12'3"

11'6"

Sinks

Vanity

Tub

Clustered sinks *serve two different compartments; doors connect to bathing space.*

Built-in *dressing table (above) includes lavatory, well-lighted mirror, and many drawers. Compartmentalized bath between two bedrooms gives each sister her own dressing area with lavatory; girls share the center compartment.*

Shared compartment *(left) contains a tub/shower and toilet. Supergraphic of apple green, orange, and lemon yellow circles the room, extending up a tiled wall, across the ceiling, down a Roman shade, and along the carpet. Architect: Fred Briggs; Interior Designer: Suzanne Faulkner.*

Special types of baths

- **Bathroom gardens**
- **Outdoor tubs and showers**
- **Japanese baths**
- **Steambaths and saunas**

Once your house is equipped with one or two standard bathrooms, your thinking may turn to more unusual types of bathing rooms.

One of the most popular ways to make a bathroom special is to use plants. You could add an extra dimension to a utilitarian bathroom by making it into a greenhouse-bathroom; or, using an attractive planting just outside the bathroom, you could create a "garden bathroom."

You may decide that you prefer to move completely out of the house and into the garden for your bathing or showering. An outdoor tub or shower can be used the year around in mild climates.

Look to the customs of other cultures for new ideas in bathing and bathrooms. The Finnish sauna, Turkish steambath, and Japanese soaking tub are all delightful ways to clean up and to unwind at the same time.

Open your bathroom to plants

A garden setting is a logical one for the bathroom— we associate greenery and flowers with relaxation. In some instances a garden is located outside the bathroom and viewed through a window or door; in others, the garden area is actually a part of the bathroom.

An exterior garden

A glass wall overlooking a patio or a sliding glass door opening from the bathroom to a private garden makes a room seem larger and more luxurious. Even an interior bathroom can look into an atrium. If a glass panel is to be located next to a shower or tub, though, it probably should be thermal glass to prevent cracking on cold days when hot water hits the glass. Thermal glass will also keep the bathroom warmer than a single sheet of glass.

Screens, fences, and plantings can be combined to provide the necessary privacy for a bathroom garden. The garden itself may be large enough for sunbathing, or it may be so small that it offers only the enjoyment of seeing a few select plantings from the bathroom. The fence can serve as a decorative background for climbing plants.

Plants for a bathroom patio or garden should be selected for their good looks and their ability to grow in a confined space. Choose plants that will thrive with a minimum of care in the environment provided for them. The climate will dictate plant choices for outside gardens. Consider how the garden will look during each season; some gardens that look interesting in spring and summer look bleak in fall and winter.

If the bath garden is entirely secluded, it can be enhanced with outdoor lighting to keep a large expanse of glass from appearing black and cold. Or draperies could be installed if the glass wall is away from shower spray.

Access to the garden for maintenance can be through a gate in the garden fence. This makes tending the garden easier and eliminates having to carry garden supplies or soil through the house to reach the bathroom garden.

Wooden framework *outside window displays plants, solves privacy problem. Box-like frame of 2 by 4s, nailed to wall studs from exterior, rests on concrete piers. Spaced 2 by 2s fastened to framework filter light.*

Step out *of tub or shower here and you have the pleasant sensation of being outdoors. Louvered, bifold doors open to garden enclosed by wood fence; insect screening covers the top. Architects: Belt Collins & Assoc. Ltd.*

Plants inside the bathroom

Moisture and humidity make bathrooms ideal for growing many types of plants. One approach is to have the plants growing in containers and arranged to present a gardenlike setting. Another is to have a permanent planter area where the plants are set directly into soil or in pots sunk into the soil. With a permanent planter, it's advisable to confine the soil to avoid continual cleaning. A glass divider, similar in construction to one wall of a shower enclosure, can be used to separate a garden area; it needn't reach to the ceiling because plants benefit from the moisture that comes from the bathing area.

If you have a partitioned bathroom, humidity levels will vary in the different compartments, a factor to consider in arranging plants. Then, too, the humidity level in a bathroom fluctuates during the day—especially if no one is at home for hours at a stretch. But since the bathroom is likely to be the most humid room in the house, remember to avoid plants (such as cactus) that require dry conditions.

Bathrooms usually have plenty of artificial illumination. In a windowless bathroom, you may have to leave the lights on all day for the sake of your plants. Unless you have lots of bright sunlight, consider shade tolerance when selecting plants.

At night, cool temperatures—as much as 20° lower than daytime temperatures—will allow plants to complete their sugar processing cycle. Plants whose temperature requirements are similar should be grouped together in indoor gardens.

(Continued on next page)

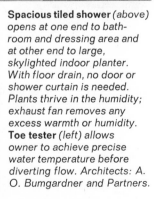

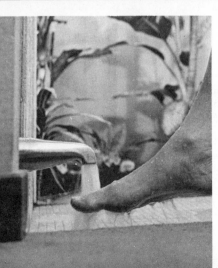

Spacious tiled shower *(above) opens at one end to bathroom and dressing area and at other end to large, skylighted indoor planter. With floor drain, no door or shower curtain is needed. Plants thrive in the humidity; exhaust fan removes any excess warmth or humidity.*
Toe tester *(left) allows owner to achieve precise water temperature before diverting flow. Architects: A. O. Bumgardner and Partners.*

These plants thrive in bathrooms

A sunny, humid bathroom can be the best environment in the house for nurturing plants. But each bathroom will offer slightly different growing conditions. Most bathrooms are a bit warmer than the rest of the house and have a comparatively lower light level and a higher, but varying, humidity level.

The following plants are suited to the conditions in an average bathroom. For detailed information on how to grow them, refer to the *Sunset* gardening books.

Aglaonema (includes Chinese evergreen)
Ardisia crenata (coral berry)
Aspidistra elatior (cast-iron plant)
Asplenium (includes mother fern, bird's nest fern)
Begonia (foliage varieties)
Callisia elegans (striped inch plant)
Cissus (includes grape ivy, dwarf kangaroo ivy)
Coffea arabica (coffee tree)
Colocasia esculenta (taro, elephant's ear)
Columnea
Ctenanthe
Cyrtomium falcatum (holly fern)
Dieffenbachia (dumb cane, mother-in-law plant)
Guzmania lingulata
Hedyscepe canterburyana

Howeia (Kentia palm)
Hypoestes sanguinolenta
Maranta leuconeura (prayer plant, rabbit tracks)
Monstera deliciosa (split-leaf philodendron)
Nertera granadensis (bead plant)
Nidularium innocentii
Pellaea (cliff brake, button fern)
Peperomia
Philodendron
Phoenix roebelenii (pigmy date palm)
Plectranthus (Swedish ivy)
Polypodium aureum (hare's foot fern)
Polystichum
Rhaphidophora aurea (devil's ivy, silver pothos)
Rhapis (lady palm)
Rhipsalidopsis gaertneri (Easter cactus)
Rhipsalis paradoxa (rice cactus)
Rhoeo spathacea (Moses-in-the-cradle)
Ruellia makoyana (trailing velvet plant)
Sansevieria (bowstring hemp, snake plant)
Saxifraga (includes strawberry geranium)
Selaginella (moss fern, spike moss)
Sparmannia africana (African linden)
Spathiphyllum
Syngonium podophyllum (arrowhead plant)
Tradescantia fluminensis (wandering Jew)

(Continued from page 69)

The best light for plants comes from the east or west. South is brighter in winter, but prolonged direct sunlight from this direction is too much for some plants.

One of the most popular places for plants in a bathroom is in front of a window. Window shelves take up very little room, the plants act as a screen, and light filtering through green leaves gives a dappling effect that's very pleasant. One easy way to place plants in the window is to build or attach brackets that will support glass shelves; glass allows light to pass through to plants on lower shelves. Plants shouldn't touch the window glass.

If floor space in the bathroom is generous, try some larger plants. A single large plant in an attractive container can be an important decorative element.

If your floor space is limited, there's always the ceiling. Hang plants on a variety of levels for maximum effect and good air circulation.

The counter top and the top of the toilet tank are other possible plant locations if the light is sufficient. If it's not, you could build glass shelves closer to a light source. If you have a free-standing sink, there's probably space underneath it for a few plants. Because corners and areas close to walls are fairly free from traffic problems, they are possible plant locations. In these locations, again, light source must be considered.

You could even keep plants in the shower—try hanging one or two from the curtain rod or build a high shelf along one wall. Most plants will enjoy the hot, wet air, but you will have to keep hot water from reaching

(Continued on page 72)

Raised planter (above) brings foliage 26 inches closer to eye level. Open bottom allows good drainage. **Each side** (left) of twin washbasin island opens to raised planter. Architects: Johnson and Perkins.

Stepped benches made of redwood hold a variety of indoor plants behind shower.

Grouped beside sunken tub, plants benefit from indirect light. Insulated, white-painted wall affords privacy and shields plants from harsh, direct sunlight. Architect: Richard Caviness.

(Continued from page 70)

them and bruising the foliage or causing rot.

Any of the things that make a bathroom appear lighter and brighter will help your plants. Light-colored walls and ceiling, large expanses of mirror, fluorescent lighting designed for plants as well as for people—all these will expand your choice of plant candidates and improve your chances of success with them.

Put a shower outside

Move a shower out under the sun in the garden and you transform the daily showering routine into a special pleasure. Showers located outside the house are particularly convenient if there's a swimming pool on the property. They're also useful for cleaning up after working in the yard and for washing sand or mud off children before they come inside.

The cost of an outdoor shower depends on the distance from the water source and the layout of the house (running pipe through a crawl space is far easier than digging a trench). An outside shower often is located near the plumbing runs for an inside bathroom, laundry, or kitchen to reduce the plumbing installation costs.

Fashion a simple outside shower from a garden hose attached above head level on a fence or a wall of the house. You can attach a shower head to the end of the hose or adjust a regular garden hose nozzle to give a spray effect. Hot and cold water can't be mixed in such a shower unless special provision is made.

The easiest plumbed shower to install would be a single-faucet, cold-water fixture, but the shower will be used much more often if you pipe hot water to it.

An outdoor shower can be mounted on almost any vertical exterior structure—house or garage wall, fence, pool cabana, or post set out in the open. The most important factor is to choose a site that drains quickly; otherwise you'll have puddles and a muddy area.

A lawn can serve for the drainage floor—if the shower doesn't receive heavy use, the soap suds and extra water won't bother it. A concrete slab, wooden duck-boards, or bricks set in sand are better, if adequately drained. But if you expect the shower to be used often, you may need to install a drain.

Projecting flat stones *serve as soap shelf and towel hook for shower on outside wall of laundry. Stonework was laid around roughed-in plumbing, fixtures were added, cement grout was applied.*

Cavorting young ladies *wash off sand under shower on beach house wall. Concrete slab floor slopes to gutter on one side. Architect: Judith Chafee.*

Double-use shower *has comfortable bench for foot washing. Designers: Belt, Collins & Associates.*

Water swirls in hydromassage bath located on deck next to swimming pool. Architect: Dale Bergerson.

Two-part bath cover (left) serves as tabletop for deck picnic, removes for a hot dip. Bench seat angles around deck; lights are hidden behind bench facing.
Lid lifts off (below) to reveal roomy 4 by 8-foot redwood bath. Deck covers plumbing. Landscape Architects: Arutunian / Kinney.

Water can drain into a rock-filled sump deep enough to carry water and soap residue away from the house and garden, but many building codes require draining to the sewer system. It's also possible to use a swimming pool drain.

You'll have to drain the shower system every year in cold-winter areas.

You can achieve privacy through plantings (a row of hedge plants works well), a short length of fence, or a roll-down curtain or blind. If the house site is windy, try to place the shower where it's protected from breezes. Or set up a wind screen.

Outdoor tubs

Designed for sitting, soaking, and relaxing close to nature, outdoor tubs are very like Japanese baths moved out of the house. Most tubs are near indoor or outdoor showers where the actual scrubbing takes place before you enter the tub.

The tubs are constructed of wood, fiberglass, or concrete. You can buy them in several standard sizes from water tank and spa dealers. Code restrictions on such tubs vary widely from community to community. If you call a wooden one a pool rather than a tub or line it with waterproof plastic, it might be approved in the stricter areas. A portable, above-ground tub is not assessable for property taxes.

An outdoor tub must be built on a strong foundation to support its substantial weight when filled. Two sturdy 4-by-4-inch joists atop four concrete piers set into solid ground will usually serve the purpose.

Equipment for operating the tub includes a pump, a filter, and a heater; a hydromassage unit is a nice extra. The machinery is often composed of standard swimming pool accessories or salvaged parts and may be hidden out of sight underneath a deck.

A typical large tub's needs: 1) Pump; 1 horsepower with leaf trap, connected to the tub by 2-inch pipe. 2) Filter; diatomaceous earth type, rated for 10,000-gallon capacity. Water should be circulated through the filter at least two hours a day; an automatic timer would be helpful. 3) Heater; 150,000 BTU "instantaneous" type. An immersion thermostat keeps the water at a steady 90° "holding" temperature to avoid a lengthy heating period before the bath; a thermostat-override switch allows the temperature to be raised for bathing. You'll probably prefer it around 110° at first, hotter later on. The thermostat uses 24 volts of power from a step-down transformer.

A hydromassage unit mounted just outside the tub rim would connect to the filter via a 1½-inch pipe. You can adjust the jet with a directional nozzle.

A ¾-inch pipe diverts water from the pump-to-filter line to the heater, from which it returns directly to the tub. If you use plastic pipe, support it well to prevent heat sag. Add fresh water to the system by a hose or by connecting the heater return pipe to the household water system. For cleaning, you can empty the tub through a T-valve just outside the drain. When not in use, the tub should be kept covered to help maintain the holding temperature, to keep leaves out, and for safety.

Bathing the Japanese way

To the Japanese, a bath is more than just a quick cleansing. It's also a form of relaxation, a ritual—sometimes a family affair.

Traditionally, the bather soaps, scrubs, and rinses himself before he enters a tub to soak in hot water up to his neck. The ritual begins as the bather washes himself thoroughly with water from the *oke* (small wooden bucket) while seated on a *koshikake* (wooden stool). After rinsing with the remaining water from the oke (the water goes down a drain in the floor), he slips very slowly into the steaming hot *furo* (tub) until he's submerged up to his chin. Extremely hot water can be tolerated if entered slowly.

Japanese tubs traditionally are made of wood. The tub is kept full of water so the wood won't dry out and expand and contract. In some areas building inspectors have approved wooden tubs; in others they haven't. Approval lies with the individual building authority, and you might want to appeal a negative decision.

Soaking tubs are available in fiberglass-reinforced plastic, or you could have one built of ceramic tile.

There are two philosophies in the construction of Japanese tubs. According to one, the tub is a piece of

Hydromassage unit *is included in contemporary version of furo. Drain control sits on tiled ledge. Architects: Bain & Overturf.*

Round *fiberglass soaking tub, tucked between shower stall and tiled bench, is fitted with whirlpool jets. Designer: Prudence Ducich.*

Serene indoor garden *next to sunken* furo *completes tiled bath that has floor drain. Architects: John Russell Rummell & Associates.*

furniture that stands free in a bathroom provided with waterproof floor and walls. According to the other, it's a built-in fixture, watertight in itself.

If you're building a new bathroom specifically to include a Japanese bath, you could install a drain in the bathroom floor to rinse away soapy water. Otherwise, the preliminary washing can be done in a shower.

Steam baths

Steam bathing, another centuries-old custom, can also be enjoyed at home. A wet heat and steam bath can be incorporated into a new or existing bathroom.

You can add a steam generator or a boiler to an ordinary bathtub area or shower stall to convert it to a steam room. You must include jets to distribute the steam throughout the enclosure.

Tub and shower stall steam baths don't interfere with other bathing functions, but they must be enclosed with specially-designed sliding glass doors (or hinged doors on shower stalls) that confine the steam to the enclosed interior. Following a steam bath, cold shower spray will dissipate the steam, condensing it into water.

Freestanding *redwood furo with dadoed joints is equipped with Japanese bathing paraphernalia, including sekken nose (soap stand).*

Sunk 5 feet deep *(above), tub has copper tubing concealed in walls to retain heat. Oak bench resists water and steam.*
In same compartment *(right), shower sports three shower heads. Architect: Tracy Price.*

Typical *prefabricated sauna built into interior of house has electric heater, smooth-finished wood surfaces. Headrests, lounge pads make saunas more comfortable. Designer: Sal Iniguez.*

Saunas: a way to fitness

The Finnish sauna is a method of bathing that's physically restorative. To benefit from this dry heat bath, you don't have to undergo as strenuous a procedure as a Finn, who completes his sauna by plunging through a hole in an ice-covered lake or rolling in a snowbank. You'll find a cold shower will do just as well.

The key to a sauna is dryness, which enables the body to withstand heat ranging from 180° to 240°. (A few drops of water on heated rocks is enough to change the humidity in the sauna.) The dry heat induces perspiration rapidly and without enervation. After cooling—suddenly, with a plunge in cold water; or gradually, at outside temperature—you experience a feeling of thorough well-being. A rest after a sauna is

advisable. Persons with high blood pressure or cardiac conditions should use the sauna only with the advice of a doctor.

A sauna can be inside the house or in a separate building, occupying a space as small as 5 by 8 feet with a 7-foot ceiling. One might fit, for example, in the space of two back-to-back wardrobe closets. A sauna is best located near a bathroom or shower and near a place where you can lie down afterward.

Gas and electric sauna heaters warm the sauna within 20 minutes to a half-hour and are equipped with adjustable thermostats to maintain their heat. Wood-burning heaters take considerably longer to heat up. With an electric heater, no plumbing or outside venting is needed, so the sauna can be located in an inside room of your house. Electric heaters require 220-volt wiring. Gas heaters require gas piping and an outside vent; wood-burning heaters also require an outside vent.

The simplest type of sauna heater doesn't depend on rocks; it has an air-circulating fan and produces constant temperature and humidity in a dry-heat room. Other sauna heaters include rocks to retain and radiate heat; you pour a few drops of water onto the rocks for a touch of high humidity at the end of the sauna. Some elaborate saunas include facilities for washing inside the sauna in the super-heated air, as the Finns do.

Manufactured, prefabricated saunas are available in various styles. Some are free-standing; others are intended to be built in. Dealers sell packages complete with heaters—such accessories as buckets, scoops, and timers are available.

Wood such as aspen, pine, or redwood is usually used in saunas to diffuse the heat so the surfaces remain warm but not hot (unless they get wet). The wood used in constructing a sauna should be well seasoned and free from knots or other imperfections. Nails should be inset or concealed (as in blind nailing or tongue-and-groove paneling); they get painfully hot to the touch.

Saunas can be simply built with ordinary stud-wall construction. Use foil-faced mineral batt insulation to fill the cavities between wall studs and between ceiling joists, leaving an air space for heat reflection between the foil and the sauna's interior paneling. Or use mineral insulation to fill the cavities, with a continuous vapor barrier of aluminum foil placed over the insulation and the studs and joists, under the wall paneling. Doors should be solid-core wood or insulated, and windows should be double glazed. A concrete floor with a drain is indicated where more than a dipper of water at a time is to be used. Since a concrete floor remains relatively cool, it is sometimes covered with wood slats.

The sauna heater can be located anywhere in the room; however, it should be placed opposite the two vents that are required to bring fresh air into the room. An electric heater cannot be recessed in the wall; it must be either free-standing or surface mounted. Most building codes require a wall covering of asbestos-cement board adjacent to a gas heater.

Sauna benches are often 24 inches wide and 18 inches high for the lower bench and (if two are used) 36 inches high for the upper. The higher the bench, the higher the temperature.

Inside sauna (above), asbestos-cement wall panel protects wall next to heater; concrete covers floor.
Focal point of deck (left), T-shaped bathhouse contains sauna. Deck provides after-sauna resting place. Landscape Architect: Anthony Guzzardo.

Adjacent bathroom lets you alternate using sauna and cooling off with a shower.

Like a busy carwash with water coming from every direction, copper-piped shower just outside sauna has three heads, each with its own control valve. Designer: Al Garvey.

Smooth, sealed, *4-inch-thick* concrete walls and floor actually contain the water in cedar-paneled bathtub.

Translucent skylight *recessed in roof over tub illuminates plants on ledge and hanging from ceiling.*

A glossary of useful terms

Aerator. Small device that mixes air with water as water flows out of the spout; minimizes splashes.

Bath, receptor. A small, low tub, occupying about the same floor area as a large shower, designed to be used primarily as a shower base or a child's bath.

Bath, recessed. A tub designed to be enclosed by walls on three sides.

Bidet. A small tub for washing the perineal area.

Brass. Generic term in the plumbing industry for fittings, regardless of the material of which they're made.

Brass, solid. Fittings in which all metal parts are brass. Surface may be chrome-plated in either a brushed or polished finish. Also called "all brass."

Cast iron, enameled. Fixture material; iron is cast in one piece and then enameled while red-hot so enamel fuses to the cast iron.

China, vitreous. Compounded ceramic material fired at high temperature; resistant to corrosion and discoloration; used for fixtures.

Code, plumbing. Rules established by a sanitation authority to regulate materials and methods of installing plumbing.

Diverter valve. Valve that changes water flow from one outlet to another, such as from a tub/shower's bath spout to the shower head.

Drain. A pipe carrying waste water in a house drainage system.

Enamel. Glasslike finish for vitreous china, cast-iron, and formed steel fixtures. Resists damage from acid substances.

Fiberglass. A material used for fixtures; a lamination of liquid polyester resins interspersed with thin glass fibers.

Fittings. Mechanical devices for the control of water entering or leaving the fixture—for instance, faucets, spouts, drain controls, diverter valves for tubs and lavatories.

Fitting, centerset. A single-unit lavatory fitting (containing handles and spout) that is surface mounted on top ledge of a lavatory or on a counter. Mounting holes are customarily 4 inches center-to-center.

Fixtures, plumbing. Devices such as tubs, toilets, and lavatories that receive water or make it available or receive liquid or water-borne waste and discharge the wastes into a drainage system.

Float valve. A device that automatically regulates the amount of water in a toilet flush tank. Also referred to as a "ball cock."

Flush valve. A device for flushing toilets or similar fixtures.

Half-bathroom. Bathroom equipped with lavatory and toilet only; without tub or shower.

Lavatory. A fixture that makes water available for washing the hands and face. Also called "wash-basin." In the plumbing industry, the word "sink" is applied to the kitchen fixture.

Ledge back. A flat elevation at the back of a lavatory, less than 2 inches above the rim and usually extending the full length of the fixture. Brass fittings are customarily mounted on the ledge.

Overflow. Outlet for escape of water in a tub or lavatory to prevent flooding of bathroom if water is left on.

Pipe, fixture supply. The pipe that brings water from behind the wall to a

Pine enclosure (above), trimmed with redwood molding and finished with spar varnish, frames standard tub. English buffet (left) makes unusual lavatory cabinet. Track lights reflect in mirror. Architect: Peter Choate.

On warm days, sliding glass door opens wide. Shower curtain pulls around tub along track recessed in ceiling. Designer: James Casella.

plumbing fixture. Also called "supply."

Pipe, soil. A pipe that carries the discharge from toilets and often from the other fixtures, too. Often called "soil stack."

Pipe, vent. A pipe installed to provide a flow of air to or from a drainage system or to provide a circulation of air within such a system, protecting trap seals from siphonage and back pressure.

Pipe, waste. A line that carries the discharge from any fixture except toilets and conveys the waste to the building drain or waste stack.

Pressure regulator. Installed between house plumbing and main water supply to regulate water pressure.

Rim, antisplash. Lip on inside front of vitreous china lavatory; minimizes water splashing out of the bowl.

Roughing in. The installation of concealed piping (in walls and floor) to which supply lines and drain from a plumbing fixture are attached.

Self-rimming. Lavatory designed for counter installation without metal mounting frame.

Shelf back. A flat elevation at the back of a lavatory, higher than 2 inches above the rim and extending the full fixture length.

Siphon jet. The most expensive and efficient type of toilet.

Spout, diverter. Tub filler spout (part of a bath and shower fitting) in which a knob is lifted to divert water from the spout to the shower head.

Stack. A general term for the main vertical pipe of a system of soil, waste, or vent piping.

Steel, enameled formed. A material for fixtures;

sheets of steel are formed and finished with baked-on porcelain enamel.

Supply. The pipe that brings water from behind the wall to a plumbing fixture.

Trap. A bent pipe section or other device that holds a water deposit and forms a seal against the passage of sewer gases.

Vacuum breaker. A device to prevent waste water backflow into a water-supply line.

Valve seat, integral. A pipe venting a trap or waste pipe beneath or behind a fixture served by it, and connected to the main vent at a point above the fixture.

Vent stack. A vertical pipe, sometimes called the main vent, that provides circulation of air to and from any part of the drainage system.

Waste. Fitting through

which water from bath or lavatory flows into waste pipe.

Waste, chain and stopper. Water is retained in basin or tub by means of a rubber stopper. Stopper chain is usually attached to the spout.

Waste, pop-up. A mechanically operated metal stopper that retains water in the basin or tub.

Waste, trip lever. Tub stopper that prevents the flow of water out of the pipe below the tub by means of a plunger. Top of waste is covered by a strainer.

Water closet. Toilet. Abbreviated "W.C."

Wet venting. Plumbing system in which one vertical pipe is used for both venting and draining waste water.

Wet wall. Wall containing supply lines and soil and waste pipes.

Index

Photographers

Edward Bigelow: 33, 34 (bottom right), 35, 36 (bottom right), 37, 38 (bottom left, bottom right), 39, 40 (left, bottom), 41 (top right), 42 (right), 43 (top left, top right, bottom left), 44 (top left, top right, bottom left), 45 (left), 46 (left), 47 (top left, bottom left), 48 (top left, bottom), 51 (center left), 52 (top left, top right, bottom left), 53 (top), 57 (top), 60, 74 (bottom left), 76, back cover (top left, bottom left). **Paul Bjornn:** 43 (bottom right). **Jeremiah O. Bragstad:** 36 (top right). **Ernest Braun:** 66 (left), 77 (top left, top right). **Glenn Christiansen:** 34 (top left), 42 (left), 73 (top), back cover (top right). **David Cornwell:** 74 (bottom right). **Robert Cox:** 29. **Dick Dawson:** 54 (top center), 57 (center left). **Walt Dibblee:** 18. **Richard Fish:** 14 (center left), 45 (bottom right), 46 (bottom right), 48 (top right), 49, 52 (bottom right), 53 (center), 61 (bottom right), 65 (top), 67, 75 (top right, bottom right), 79 (left, center). **Roger Flanagan:** 57 (bottom). **Gerald Fredrick:** 27, 59 (top). **Art Hupy:** 14 (bottom right). **Leonard Koren:** 14 (top). **Edmund Y. Lee:** 63 (bottom). **Leland Y. Lee:** 44 (bottom right). **Fred Lyon:** 43 (top center). **Philip Molten:** 43 (center left), 47 (top right). **Stewart Morton:** 36 (bottom left). **Michael D. Moyer:** 32. **Nelson/Zellers:** 66 (right). **Don Normark:** 41 (bottom left), 54 (top right), 57 (top left), 61 (bottom left), 63 (top), 65 (center), 69 (top left, bottom left), 72 (top right), 74 (top left). **Norman A. Plate:** 8 (right), 17, 34 (top right), 40 (top), 61 (top left, top center, top right), 71 (top right, bottom right), 78 (left). **Martha Rosman:** 51 (bottom right), 53 (bottom), 64. **Hal Ross:** 8 (left). **Augie Salbosa:** 51 (top), 75 (bottom left). **Darrow M. Watt:** 13, 15, 31, 36 (top left), 38 (top right), 46 (top right), 51 (bottom left), 52 (bottom center), 54 (left, bottom right), 59 (bottom), 63 (center), 69 (top center), 72 (left), 73 (center, bottom), 77 (bottom left, bottom right), 78 (right), 79 (right). **Robert Wenkam:** 19, 72 (bottom right). **Wenkam/Salbosa:** 69 (top right), 71 (top left, center left). **Michael Wright:** 38 (center). **Craig Zwicky:** 7.